Fly

Animal

Series editor: Jonathan Burt

Already published

Crow
Boria Sax

Ant
Charlotte Sleigh

Tortoise
Peter Young

Cockroach
Marion Copeland

Dog
Susan McHugh

Oyster
Rebecca Stott

Bear
Robert E. Bieder

Rat
Jonathan Burt

Snake
Drake Stutesman

Parrot
Paul Carter

Bee
Claire Preston

Tiger
Susie Green

Whale
Joe Roman

Falcon
Helen Macdonald

Peacock
Christine E. Jackson

Salmon
Peter Coates

Fox
Martin Wallen

Cat
Kay Rogers

Forthcoming . . .

Hare
Simon Carnell

Moose
Kevin Jackson

Crocodile
Richard Freeman

Spider
Katja and Sergiusz Michalski

Duck
Victoria de Rijke

Wolf
Garry Marvin

Elephant
Daniel Wylie

Pigeon
Barbara Allen

Horse
Elaine Walker

Penguin
Stephen Martin

Rhinoceros
Kelly Enright

Fly

Steven Connor

REAKTION BOOKS

Published by
REAKTION BOOKS LTD
33 Great Sutton Street
London EC1M 3JU, UK

www.reaktionbooks.co.uk

First published 2006

Printed and bound in Singapore by CS Graphics

British Library Cataloguing in Publication Data
Connor, Steven, 1955–
    Fly. – (Animal)
    1. Flies 2. Human ecology - History
    I.Title
    595.7'7

ISBN-13: 978 186189 294 2
ISBN-10: 1 86189 294 2

Contents

1 Fly Familiar

Am not I
À fly like thee?
Or art not thou
A man like me?
William Blake, 'The Fly'

More than the rat, the cat, the dog or the horse, the fly is our familiar. Flies accompany human beings wherever they go, and have probably done so since the first development and spread of animal husbandry among early humans. Flies are, as one of their rare celebrants has written, 'the constant, immemorial witnesses to the human comedy'.[1] Flies were indeed literally thought to be the 'familiars' of witches. But flies are familiar in another sense. For what we might call the *Gestalt* or footprint of the fly extends far beyond its most familiar forms, such as the house fly. About one tenth of all the species known to science are flies. Not only this, many creatures that are not flies at all have nevertheless been given the name: dragonflies, butterflies and fireflies; even the flea has a name that factitiously suggests an association with the fly. The spellings 'flee', 'flea' and 'flie' were largely interchangeable in the volatile orthography of pre-eighteenth-century English. The word fly is used to signify any kind of small flying creature, of indeterminate form. Flies are so familiar that we allow them to multiply, in kind as well as number, under our noses.

Flies are defined biologically as insects of the order Diptera (Greek, 'two-winged'). Diptera are distinguished from other flying insects, such as dragonflies and butterflies, by having only one pair of wings. Where other flying insects have a second

An array of types of fly on a page from an early German scientific book, reproducing an earlier illustration from Ulisse Aldrovandi.

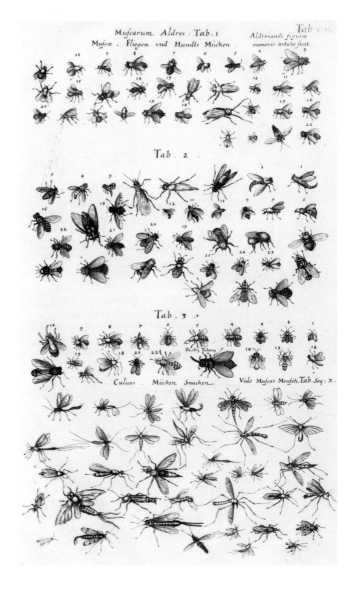

pair of wings, many Diptera have a pair of club-like balancing organs, known as halteres, named after the counterweights that Greek long-jumpers used to assist their flight through the air. The order of Diptera encompasses 29 families, among them the following: Tipulidae, or crane flies, 3,000 species of which were distinguished by the entomologist C. P. Alexander; Culicidae, or mosquitoes; Chironomidae, or midges; Tabanidae, or horse flies; Asilidae, or robber flies; Syrphidae, flower flies or hover flies; Drosopholidae, vinegar flies or fruit flies.

The most well known and widely dispersed families of Diptera, however, are the Muscidae, encompassing *Musca domestica*, the house fly, the stable-fly and the tsetse fly; Calliphoridae, or blow flies, the family that includes bluebottles;

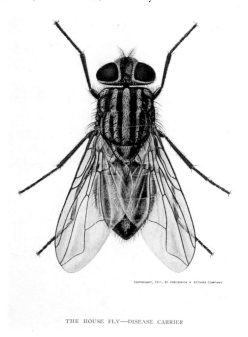

The house fly, frontispiece to L. O. Howard, *The House-Fly, Disease Carrier: An Account of Its Dangerous Activities and of the Means of Destroying It* (1911).

COPYRIGHT, 1911, BY FREDERICK A. STOKES COMPANY

THE HOUSE FLY—DISEASE CARRIER

Bluebottle
maggots.

and Sarcophagidae, or flesh flies. It is this class of Diptera that is usually meant when we refer to 'flies'. The reason for this is their feeding and breeding habits. The house fly lays its eggs in piles of dung or other decaying organic matter. The maggots that hatch from these eggs feed on the rotting matter until they pupate. The adult fly, though a promiscuous feeder, also has a taste for this kind of decaying matter. Blowflies and flesh-flies prefer to lay their eggs on dead bodies, including the bodies of humans. A sudden appearance of bluebottles (*Calliphora vicina*) in a house will usually indicate that there is a dead animal, such as a mouse or bird, somewhere at hand.

The poet John Clare took great delight in flies and rapturously celebrated their co-tenancy in human spaces, their sharing of food and human lives:

These little indoor dwellers in cottages and halls, were always entertaining to me, after dancing in the window all day from sunrise to sun-set they would sip of the tea, drink of the beer, and eat of the sugar, and be welcome all

summer long, they look like things of mind or fairries [sic], and seemed pleased or dull as the weather permits in many clean cottages, and genteel houses, they are allowed every liberty to creep, fly, or do as they like, and seldom or ever do wrong, in fact they are the small or dwarfish portion of our own family, and so many fairy familiars that we know and treat as one of ourselves.[2]

The bluebottle.

This attitude is far from typical, however. Flies may be domestic, but they are rarely seen as domesticated or homely, *heimlich*, in the way that dogs and cats or even budgerigars may be. In German, the house fly is not a *Hausfliege* but a *Stubenfliege*, 'room-fly', or, more generally, 'indoor' fly. Pliny thought no creature 'less teachable or less intelligent' than the fly and Plutarch followed this

A house fly on
a stone slab.

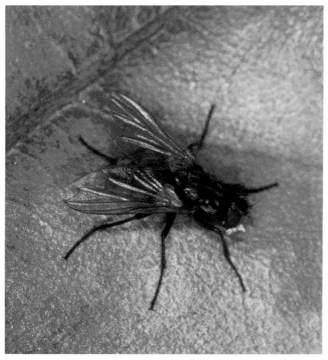

A house fly on
a leaf.

tradition in asserting that '[o]f all the creatures that share man's dwelling, the fly and swallow alone cannot be domesticated. They will not let themselves be touched or allow any companionship, or share in any task of recreation.'[3] He was wrong about the swallow, which has been trained to send messages, but the fly remains almost entirely intractable to human will and purpose. Emerson agreed that 'A fly is as untamable as a hyena.'[4] Only to the most perverse or one in the greatest extremity of solitude (the desert anchorite, the Alcatraz lifer) does it occur to make a pet of this egregious pest. As both our constant fellow-traveller and provoking other, the fly is our familiar-stranger, our dis-similar. The fly is disconcerting in its capacity to make itself at home in our vicinity or our homes. Charles Olson evokes the sense of eviction aroused by an over-familiar fly:

A big fat fly
lives in my house
and in the air
he goes about
as though in fact the house
were just as much his
as it is
mine . . .
And I am
suddenly only
a co dweller here[5]

There are no secrets to be kept from the fly. In the play *Mercator* by the Roman comic dramatist Plautus, a young man complains that he has been unable to keep his mistress concealed from his father, who is 'a a regular fly – you can't keep anything from him, there's not a corner sacred or profane but

what he's in it instantly'.[6] The fly is feared and despised not just because of its easy entrance into our houses, but because of where it has been before it arrives, dabbling its fingers, or its feet, indifferently in pâtisserie and cowpat. 'The busy fly is in every dish' goes a Spanish saying, and the sentiment is matched by the Russian 'Flies and priests can enter any house.' We suppose that the fly, unlike the priest, is bringing filth and danger into the spaces of human occupation. We will see later that suspicion and hatred of the fly have been sharpened over the last century by the discoveries and techniques of bacteriology, but the fly's habits of hopping indifferently from excrement to aliment have long made it the embodiment of spatial and categorial disturbance, bringing places that should be kept apart into promiscuous proximity with each other. Flies are vehicles, vectors, that set at naught our safe demarcation of spaces. Perhaps they are a kind of anti-angel, which spreads malaise and unease rather than good news.

The Master of Frankfurt, *The Artist and his Wife*, 1496, oil on wood.

The fly therefore represents a particular provocation for cultures and religions that attempt to maintain strong and absolute distinctions between the clean and the unclean. According to the Talmud, flies arouse disgust because of their habits of moving between filthy and clean circumstances, and flying between the sick and the healthy. The poisonous 'Egyptian fly' is regarded by the Talmud as so dangerous that, unlike other creatures, it may be killed on the Sabbath.[7] On the other hand, the very ubiquity of flies seems to have meant that they were often regarded with tolerance or resignation. The fly may spoil the ointment (in its original context in Ecclesiastes 10.1 this is through odour rather than ugliness), but a Talmudic formula suggests that, if a man finds a fly and a hair in a meal cooked by his wife, the fly can be forgiven, since it is in the nature of things, while the hair may constitute grounds for divorce. Elsewhere in the Middle East, the fly has been regarded as a useful presence, hunting down gnats and other insects, thereby making houses habitable.[8]

The horsefly (*Tabanus sudeticus*).

And yet, though flies will sometimes travel up to 15 miles (24 km) under their own steam, and can be lifted up by winds and thus be transported even further than this, for the most part they occupy quite restricted ranges – about a quarter of mile (400 m) being the average flight range. How can a stay-at-home like the house fly have become so widely diffused across the globe? It is almost certainly because of being carried by humans, in their curiosity and restless urge to conquer new territories, and being sustained by the animal upon whom humans have relied for so long for their conveyance, the horse. For centuries, flies have shared human habitations because of the rich source of nourishment provided by the various kinds of excrement, solid and liquid, human and animal, that are always so abundantly in evidence about them. Once human beings ceased to be nomadic, and settled in agricultural and then urban communities, they ceased to leave their droppings on the road. When human beings came to rest, it was their excrements that had to be mobilized, via gutters, drains, sewers and other forms of *cloacae*. So, as human beings began to farm, rather than graze the earth, flies developed an animal husbandry of their own, cultivating human beings for the decaying matter of which they proved to be such prodigiously efficient producers. As one nineteenth-century encyclopedia put it, 'The house flies is such a constant companion of man, that its presence in a coral or other island is sufficient evidence that human inhabitants are not or have not been far distant.'9 So, in a sense, while it is the fly that spreads and carries disease to humans, it is also humans who spread and carry flies. Flies and humans are reciprocal hitch-hikers. And, although flies can bring into our houses and onto our plates organisms that we would prefer to hold at a safe and hygienic distance, the restriction of their range means that what they bring back to us is mostly our own. Flies bring us disconcertingly to ourselves.

Partying vermin. 'The Martiniquan Association of Rats, Mice, Mosquitoes, Cockroaches, Flies . . . says THANK YOU.'

This is effectively dramatized in William Golding's *Lord of the Flies*, at the moment at which the mystic Simon tries to articulate to the other boys marooned on their tropical island his apprehension that 'the Beast' that they all fear might be inside them rather than somewhere outside. Golding brings together the intimacy of the first person plural with the ineffability of excrement, the two worlds that the fly effortlessly commingles:

'What I mean is . . . maybe it's only us.'

'Nuts!'

That was from Piggy, shocked out of decorum.

Simon went on.

'We could be sort of . . .'

Simon became inarticulate in his effort to express mankind's essential illness. Inspiration came to him.

'What's the dirtiest thing there is?'[10]

Flies are the enemy of the human. And yet, because they are such an intimate enemy, human beings can readily identify with the weakness and vulnerability of flies. God-mimicking man finds it easy to feel fly-like in the face of abstract divine power, hence Gloucester's remark: 'As flies to wanton boys are we to th'Gods/They kill us for their sport' (King Lear, iv. 1, 36–7). Not that flies have always been thought of simply as weak and negligible. We might say, of somebody who is bright and alert, that 'there are no flies on him', though such a person might also once himself have been called 'fly'. Indeed, in the ancient world, the fly was admired for its courage in attacking much larger opponents than itself. Horapollo, a fifth-century interpreter of Egyptian hieroglyphics, records that '[t]o indicate impudence, they draw a fly, which, when suddenly driven off, none the less comes right back'.[11] Egyptian soldiers who displayed such qualities of indomitability were rewarded with large flies made of gold or silver. Ahmose-pen-Nekhbet (fl. c. 1570–1550 BC) records in an autobiographical text that he was awarded six flies by the Pharoah Thutmose I.[12] The Cairo Museum has several such flies found with the remains of the Pharoah Ahmosis.[13] The British Museum has a necklace made of interlocking flies which may also perhaps have been awarded to recognize courage in battle and military prowess.

The fly was also admired in ancient Greece, with Homer as its most influential celebrant. In book 2 of the *Iliad*, the armed hosts of the Achaeans are described as pouring from their ships onto the plains of Scamander like flocks of cranes or geese or, in the culminating image, like 'the many tribes of swarming flies that buzz about the herdsman's farmstead in the season of spring, when the milk drenches the pails'.[14] Later, Homer has Athena give to Menelaus 'the daring of a fly that, though it be driven away often from the skin of a man, ever persists in biting, and sweet to it is the blood of man'.[15] Homer's admiration is recalled approvingly in an essay in praise of the fly by the rhetorician and satirist Lucian of Samosata (AD 120–180), who

Homer's Philoctetes waving flies away from his unhealable wound.

is impressed that so small a creature should find an approved place in the work of the most 'mighty-mouthed' (*megaphono-tatos*) of the poets.[16] He quotes some lines from a piece of tragic drama (unidentified) in which Homer's estimate of the fly's courage is repeated:

> 'Tis strange that while the fly with hardy strength
> Encounters man to sate itself with gore,
> Stout men-at-arms should fear the foeman's lance.[17]

Lucian finds other things to admire beyond the warlike capacities identified by Homer. He notes the beauty and delicacy of the fly's wings, which he says are as Indian fabrics to Greek when compared with those of grasshoppers and bees, and have the rainbow iridescence of the peacock's wings.[18] He also approves of the fact that flies are active only in the light, which means that no suspicion attaches to them of treachery or deceit: 'in the dark . . . she does nothing: she has no desire for stealthy actions and no thought of disgraceful deeds which would discredit her if they were done by daylight'.[19]

The brilliantly coloured *Alophora hemiptera*.

Lucian's ironic praise of the fly was the spur for Leon Battista Alberti (1404–1470), a Florentine humanist who wrote on many subjects, and who has sometimes been thought of as the precursor to Leonardo da Vinci in the range of his accomplishments. Alberti writes that he had been suffering from a fever when he received a Latin translation of Lucian's 'The Fly' dedicated to him by his friend Guarino. Instantly he began to revive and started to dictate his own Latin encomium to the fly. Alberti begins by enlarging the Homeric praise of the warlike qualities of the fly, which he claims is far more worthy of praise than the bee, which has been the subject of such disproportionate care and attention.[20] The fly has no settled position, but conducts its campaigns fearlessly and without remission. Preferring to spend its life in continual combat and having no sympathy for the work of fire, plunder and ruin, the fly can be seen to observe the rules of humanity and piety (p. 176). Alberti builds on Lucian's hint about the fly's abhorrence of sneakiness or stealth, to emphasize the transparency of the fly's means and manners: 'The fly passes its life in the light, in the company of men, in the theatre of the world, so to speak. Molested by nobody, content in itself, envious of nobody, it never seeks to act without the presence of a spectator' (p. 180). Even the fly's manner of eating is public and companionable, and, Alberti reminds us, 'eating together is next to love' (p. 180). Furthermore, and despite what he has earlier told us about the fly's martial prowess, Alberti insists that the fly is peace-loving, unlike other so-called sociable insects, such as bees and ants, who embark on destructive civil wars. 'How idyllic, how peaceful, how equable the lives of men would be if they conducted themselves like flies!' (p. 182).

As this picture of one fly apparently consuming another shows, flies do not always dine together as companionably as Alberti suggests.

Up to this point in the essay, Alberti's tone remans coyly balanced, allowing the reader little opportunity to take his extravagant praises of the fly at anything other than face value. With the unexpected claim that flies are also distinguished for the intensity of their religious devotion, a hairline crack appears in the elegant surface of Alberti's encomium:

> Who does not know how full of religion flies are? Has there ever anywhere been a festival in honour of the gods or any sacrifice in which flies have not taken as large a part as they could? First they sip, then leave the altar, and gather in hordes to take part in the ritual, keeping midnight vigil with the very gods [p. 184].

Because the fly misses nothing, with its enormous, all-seeing eyes, and goes everywhere, it must be credited with limitless experience and sagacity:

> The fly has known the sweets which Circe offered to change her guests into swine; knew where Osiris was hiding when everybody sought him; knew the defects of Helen's posterior, and laid hands on the hidden parts of Ganymede. It even knew the sour taste of Andromache's pendulous old breasts, on which it settled again and again [p. 184].

And yet, the fly is distinguished by its discretion: not once has it been known to divulge any of the secrets it has learned. Alberti's ironic manoeuvres here skilfully take all of the characteristics of the fly that make it seem inhuman or remote from the possibility of identification and sympathy and find, or feign to find, in them grounds for admiration.

The fly has had more modern admirers. It makes two appearances in *The Queen of the Air*, John Ruskin's meditation upon the figure of Athena and the airy virtues she represents. The first is when Ruskin, like Lucian, recalls Homer's decision to have Athena give Menelaus the courage of a fly. Ruskin praises Homer's unconscious grasp of truths that would not be unfolded scientifically until much later:

It is only recent science which has completely shown the perfectness of this minute symbol of the power of Athena; proving that the insect's flight and breath are co-ordinated; that its wings are actually forcing pumps, of which the stroke compels the thoracic respiration; and that it thus breathes and flies simultaneously by the action of the same muscles, so that respiration is carried on most vigorously during flight.[21]

When the fly makes its next appearance, much further on in *The Queen of the Air*, it is as an illustration of the principle of liberty:

There is no courtesy in him; he does not care whether it is king or clown whom he teases; and in every step of his swift mechanical march, and in every pause of his resolute observation, there is one and the same expression of perfect egotism, perfect independence and self-confidence, and conviction of the world's having been made for flies. Strike at him with your hand, and to him, the mechanical fact and external aspect of the matter is, what to you it would be if an acre of red clay, ten feet thick, tore itself up from the ground in one massive field, hovered over you in the air for a second, and came crashing down with an aim . . . He steps out of the way of your hand, and alights on the back of it. You cannot terrify him, nor govern him, nor persuade him, nor convince him [p. 123].

Ruskin settles on the very qualities of the fly that have made it difficult to bestow on it the same admiration accorded to the ant or the bee, namely, its refusal to work, build or prepare for the future:

> He has no work to do – no tyrannical instinct to obey . . .
> free in the air, free in the chamber – a black incarnation
> of caprice, wandering, investigating, flitting, flirting,
> feasting at his will, with rich variety of choice in feast,
> from the heaped sweets in the grocer's window to those
> of the butcher's back-yard, and from the galled place on
> your cab-horse's back, to the brown spot in the road,
> from which, as the hoof disturbs him, he rises with angry
> republican buzz – what freedom is like his? [pp. 123–4]

Perhaps the prominence given to the fly by Ruskin in this celebration of the goddess Athena has to do with the fact that he sees the goddess primarily as 'air as the spirit of life' (p. 328). Ruskin is not the first or last to see the fly as the embodiment as well as the denizen of the air. But it is perhaps not in its qualities of life and vigour that the fly most resembles human beings. Rather, the most telling sign of our reluctant sense of identity with the fly is the phrase 'to die like flies'. For flies also bring us close to the most intimate fact of all, that of our own certain, personal deaths. The flies that we despatch so easily and carelessly, so that they have become proverbial for the thoughtless massacre of humans, will still be there when we are no longer, or at least no longer in any state to swat them from their repast

QVASI FLOS EGREDITVR
ET CONTERITVR . ET
FVGIT VELVT VMBRA ·
· IOB · 14 ·

North German School, *Vanitas*, c. 1600, oil on wood.

(which may at that moment be us). The fly is more than a *memento mori*; its infuriating incapacity to see any significant difference between life and death makes it seem as though to the fly we may already have plenty of death about us. For the hungry fly, I am unripe carrion, or a precocious kind of corpse. 'The fly/I've just brushed/from my face keeps buzzing/about me, flesh-/eater/starved for the soul', writes Galway Kinnell in

Guercino, *Et in Arcadia Ego*, 1618, oil on canvas.

his poem 'The Fly'. Even if we manage to ignore the fly, it will be there with us at the last: 'we say our last goodbye/to the fly last,/the flesh-fly last'.[22] The grim synanthropic ring-a-roses danced out between flies and men is nicely expressed in Raymond Queneau's *Foutaises* (1944): 'When one sees flies, one thinks; *they came from maggots*. When one sees men, one thinks, *to maggots they will come*.'[23]

Flies are not so easy for humans to kill as the expression 'to die like flies' might suggest, although human beings have worked hard to devise means of exterminating them en masse. One correspondent writing to *Notes and Queries* in 1939 thought that the phrase 'dying like flies' must have its origin in some historical event, presumably since flies do not in fact die so easily or obligingly as all that.[24] But, though flies in their prime are not easy to kill, that prime is short-lived. Numberless though flies sometimes seem, the days of the individual fly are strictly numbered – fewer than a hundred, for most species. Many flies will be taken by other animals, birds, fish and frogs, as food. But a housefly who dodges the hungry beak or tongue is very likely to die in a manner that may be in gruesome congruence with our own fears about the secret knowledge it possesses of our own ultimate undoings. Towards the end of summer, flies can sometimes be found standing almost motionless, proboscis extended, but unresponsive either to a wave of the hand or nudge of the finger. Closer observation may reveal a circle of white spores around the feet of the motionless fly. Such flies may be in the final stages of infestation by a fungus, which will eventually consume them from the inside out, in just the way that the fly's maggots consume the bodies they take for their food. The action of the fungus *Empusa muscae* was first suggested by Charles de Geer in 1782 and subsequently described by Goethe in 1828 and A.M.C. Duéril in 1835. If flies live on our death, they also seem at times to be living it out, the desiccated effigies of their life-in-death recalling the fly-blown fate of our own bodies after death. 'The flies that die in the autumn are just as we are in creation', wrote Guy de Maupassant.[25]

It is perhaps this feeling for its autumnal susceptibility that produces traditions of the magical value of the last fly of winter. A 'Christmas-fly' appearing in the house in the last week of December was until recently held in different parts of England to be a blessing on the house, or a stranger come to help with the household chores, and so was not supposed to be killed.[26] We are sometimes able to turn round our own indifference to the deaths of flies into a recognition of the indifference of nature and time to our own lives and deaths, absorbing though they both seem to us. When there is identification with flies, it takes the form of an abstract identification with what is scarcely there and quickly passes away. Humans see themselves as like flies not in the same way as they might see themselves as like apes, or eagles or even ants. Humans are like flies in the same way that all flesh is grass (Isaiah 40.6). Blake compares human life to that of a fly in *Songs of Experience*:

> Little Fly
> Thy summers play,
> My thoughtless hand
> Has brush'd away.
>
> Am not I
> A fly like thee?
> Or art not thou
> A man like me?
>
> For I dance
> And drink & sing:
> Till some blind hand
> Shall brush my wing.
>
> If thought is life
> And strength & breath:
> And the want
> Of thought is death;
>
> Then am I
> A happy fly,
> If I live,
> Or if I die.[27]

In what follows, I will be concerned with the figure and the figuring of the fly. But perhaps the oddity of this word lets us capture something of the fly's difficult familiarity. For the word

'The Fly', from William Blake's *Songs of Experience*, 1794.

figura means both form and face. Just as they have often seemed uncertain of form, insects, and especially flies, seem to have no discernible faces. Among the more obviously ironic items in Alberti's 'Musca' is the praise for the creature's equanimity, which leads it to endure all changes of fortune with a perfectly unchanged countenance. The thing that makes the fly so inhuman, so impossible to imagine being, in our way of being, its lack of a face, is here represented as the highest human virtue:

The unchanging
face of the
house fly.

I am ready to declare that the fly is the only creature blessed
with such equanimity that it has never anywhere been seen
to laugh, or weep, or furrow its brow, or clear its forehead in
the face of any adversity or good fortune. The set of its
features is always the same, whether in private or abroad in
public places, and it always presents itself as fly [p. 186].

The irony of Alberti's reading is that, while always so perfectly apparent and apparently self-evident, the fly never entirely or exactly 'presents itself' at all. The fly is always itself, but
that self does not form a figure, nor yet exactly figure a form.
More than anything else, the fly is a figure for this unfigurability.
The significance of the fly is that it marks the insignificant, an
ordinary but vexatious remission in the given-ness or apparent-
ness of things.

2 Musca Maledicta

Despite its familiarity (or perhaps because of it), the fly has often been taken to have magical, supernatural and even demonic associations. Freud famously begins his essay on the uncanny by observing that the German words *heimlich* and *unheimlich* (homely and unhomely) have meanings that loop together, and it may be the very homeliness of the house fly that makes it apt to take on magical or supernatural qualities.[1] Not all of these are negative. A long tradition associates the soul with the butterfly. In Greek, the word *psyche* signifies both soul and butterfly, just as *animula* in Latin can mean both little soul and butterfly. In part the figuring of the soul as butterfly confirms an almost universal tendency to view the soul as lighter and more airy than the body. As Marina Warner points out, the butterfly does more symbolic work than merely suggesting the lightness of the soul. The stages of the butterfly's life, from egg to caterpillar to chrysalis to mature insect, also suggest the refinement of the soul through metamorphosis.[2] Flies and butterflies have sometimes been associated, for example, in Edmund Spenser's poem 'Muipotmos', in which the flitting, pleasure-loving Clarion who comes to grief in a spider's web is called simply 'flie' almost throughout.[3]

The fly too has been credited with powers of resurrection. Pliny in his *Natural History* and Aelian in his second-century

Many varieties of fly – like this *Rhingia campestris* – feed on flowers, as butterflies also do.

book of anecdotes and traditions regarding various animals, *De natura animalium*, agree that, though flies drown easily and frequently, they can be revived by being sprinkled with ashes and warmed in the sun.[4] In his essay in praise of the fly, Lucian reports the same belief, reproving Plato for overlooking the fact in his discussion of the soul that

> when ashes are sprinkled on a dead fly, she revives and has a second birth and a new life from the beginning. This should absolutely convince us that the fly's soul is immortal like ours, since after leaving the body it comes back again, recognizes and reanimates it, and makes the fly take wing.[5]

Other mythical and folklore traditions attest to the fly's powers of revival or reincarnation. In the Celtic *Tochmarc Étaine*, the fairy Étaine is turned by an enemy into a fly, in which form she falls into the goblet of the wife of King Etar. The queen swallows the fly, becomes pregnant as a result, and gives birth to a reincarnated Étaine, who lives as the daughter of Etar.[6] In Malay magic, one must guard against the loss of hair or nail clippings, since they carry something of the owner's soul with them and, as one researcher reports, '[c]lippings from finger-nails can turn into fire-flies just as the soul of a whole man can turn into a firefly'.[7]

The fact that the fly has a soul twins easily with the idea that the fly is the soul, or the soul figurable as a fly. The appearance of fly-amulets as pendants on funerary necklaces in Egyptian tombs may hint at the identification of the fly and the soul. Gene Kritsky suggests that ancient Egyptians may have been disturbed by seeing flies leaving bodies that were being prepared for mummification (the process took long enough for egg-laying and breeding to occur). Believing that they might be the *ka* of the deceased leaving the body before it had been properly prepared

Flies border on the Apocalypse; St John's vision on Patmos has flies at its edge in this page from the late-15th-century *Isabella Breviary*.

for the afterlife, they fashioned amulets to restore the spirit or restrain it from leaving the body.[8] A number of Egyptian fly-amulets with human heads are known, which suggests to E. A. Wallis Budge that 'at one period the Egyptians represented the soul as a human-headed fly, just as they depicted it as a human-headed hawk'.[9] A contemporary Egyptian belief that one should not kill flies in houses, since they might be the spirit of an ancestor who lived there, may be a survival of this pattern of thought.

However, where the butterfly suggests the aspiration and freedom of the completed soul, the fly often suggests some kind of displacement or imperfection. In '2 Flies' Charles Bukowski describes two angry flies buzzing round his room as 'loose chunks of soul/left out of somewhere' and, later on in the poem, '*unholiness*'.[10] The word 'unholiness' is secularized in Bukowski's poem, in which it is the literal failure to add up or cohere that is emphasized. But the association of the fly with decomposition seems to make it apt to express the discomposure of soul and body across many periods and cultures. Thus the fly tends to represent or be associated with the mischievous or baleful powers of the spirit. A story from Malawi tells of two labourers who, finding themselves unable to wake their sleeping employer, suspect her of being a witch who has sent her soul abroad to perform mischief. When a large fly wobbles by, they capture it, believing it to be the woman's soul. But it escapes, and flies into the gaping woman's mouth, at which point she awakes.

Flies have long been thought to have demonic attributes or associations. Jean Bodin, author of one of the most influential books on witchcraft and sorcery of the sixteenth century, explained that 'God wished to weaken Satan, and so gave him power ordinarily and primarily over less exalted creatures, like serpents, or flies, and other animals which the Law of God calls unclean'.[11] Elsewhere, Bodin repeats stories of the powers over flies possessed by pagan gods.

> Beelzebub . . . means Lord of the flies, on account of the fact that not a single fly was to be found in his temple, as is also said of the Palace at Venice, and the Palace at Toledo, where equally not a single one is to be found, which is neither a strange, nor new thing: for we read that, after the Cyrenians had sacrificed to the god Acharon, God of flies, and the Greeks to Jupiter Myoides, which is to say Fly-hunter, which they did every year in the month of May, all the flies flew away in a cloud.[12]

Bodin also sees witches and sorcerers as a kind of vermin, which one can never hope entirely to extirpate: 'not that it is possible to drive out all sorcerers, for there will always be some of them, who resemble toads, grass-snakes, spiders in houses and the flies of the air, which are engendered from corruption and which draw poison from the earth and infection from the air'.[13]

We might find the beginning of the association between demons and flies in the early years of the Christian era, when the Church was trying to assert its authority against competing

The 'plague of flies' from Exodus 8 features in the Christian trading-card game *Redemption*.

and soon to be superseded religions. In the *City of God* St Augustine answers an argument from adherents of Roman religion that the gods had abandoned Rome because of the coming of Christianity. Rather, he says, it is the immorality of the citizens which 'by their evil ways, had already driven all these numerous little gods away from the city's altars like so many flies'.[14] In both cases, the comparison between demons and flies is intended to suggest a diminution of the power of evil. But sometimes the fly-associations work in the other direction, amplifying the frightening powers of devils. Describing a job he once had corpse-watching in Thessaly, Thelyphron, in Apuleius' second-century Latin novel of metamorphoses, *The Golden Ass*, explains that the bodies of the newly dead have to be guarded to prevent witches getting at them: 'These dreadful creatures, who can change themselves into anything, will take on the shape of any animal you like to name and creep up on you in stealth . . . They can take on the form of birds or dogs or mice or even flies.'[15] Ben Jonson's *The Alchemist* begins with a list of the frauds practised by the group of cozeners at its centre, among which is 'selling flies', by which is meant familiar spirits. Insects may suggest themselves as suitable forms for the devil to adopt, not just because insects are regarded as creeping and unclean, but also because of the transformations that they visibly undergo. Indeed, John Webster, writing in 1677 against the belief in witchcraft, uses the existence of such natural metamorphosis to give leverage to his argument against the power of devils to suspend natural laws:

> There are natural Transformations by progression to perfection, as is manifest in Insects, which at the first to our view do appear to be Worms, Maggots, Creepers, or Caterpillers, and yet afterwards do become several sorts of winged Creatures, as Butterflies of many and various kinds, Flies, and the like . . . These being natural Transfigurations (for so they may be properly called) we cannot rationally suppose that any man of judgment will imagine, that any such can be produced by Devils or Witches, because they are brought forth by natural Principles and Agents, which Devils or Witches cannot over-rule, alter, nor hinder.[16]

The smallness and insignificance of flies made them a useful form for demons to adopt to effect their comings and goings surreptitiously. Aramaic magic texts to keep at bay the demon Lilith, whose special province was childbirth and its complications, suggest that Lilith could enter the rooms of pregnant women as a fly.[17] Balthasar Bekker wrote that the devil 'can sometimes go and come, enter into Man, and come out invisibly, and sometimes, also visibly and under the figures of small

Beasts, or insects, as Ants, Flies, Spiders, or under those little birds'.[18] Martin Del Rio went into more detail, explaining the usefulness to the devil of being able to take on the shape of a fly: 'If there are people present who prevent him conferring with his agents, or from whom he wishes to remain concealed, he changes himself into a fly and, drawing near to their ears, whispers to them of his wishes.'[19] The devil's power over flies transmogrifies into the belief, recorded by Montague Summers, that vampires are able to command flies (the association may also be assisted by the sanguineous intermediary between vampire and fly, the mosquito).[20]

A witchcraft trial in Bury St Edmunds in 1664 included an account of a bewitched child called Deborah Pacey, who was tormented by evil spirits in the form of, among other creatures, flies 'which brought crooked Pins into her, and made her first swallow them, and then vomit them'.[21] A priest named Pierre Aupetit from the French village of Fossas confessed that he had for many years been a sorcerer in the service of Beelzebub, who had given him the power to cure the sick. He testified to the authorities 'that when he was going to cure the sick, the Devil appeared to him in the form of a large fly and instructed him in what he must do, and spoke to him certain unknown words from a language he knew not'.[22] One of the most widely publicized cases of witchcraft in the seventeenth century involved a woman called Elizabeth Style. We have an unusually detailed knowledge of this case due to the transcriptions of testimony and affidavits provided by Joseph Glanvill. Nicholas Lambert, one of the three men appointed by the Justice to watch over Style, gave remarkably concrete evidence of the belief in flies as evil spirits:

about Three of the Clock in the Morning, there came from her Head a glistering bright Fly, about an Inch in length, which pitched at first in the Chimney, and then vanished. In less than a quarter of an hour after, there appeared two Flies more of a loos size, and another colour, which seemed to strike at the Examinants hand, in which he held his Book, but missed it, the one going over, the other under at the same time. He looking stedfastly then on *Style*, perceived her Countenance to change, and to become very black and gastly, the Fire also at the same time changing its colour; whereupon the Examinant, *Thick* and *Read* conceiving that her Familiar was then about her, looked to her Poll, and seeing her Hair shake very strangely took it up, and then a Fly like a great Millar [a name applied to a number of flying insects of white or powdery appearance, including the cockchafer and the ghost-moth *Hepialus humuli*] flew out from the place, and pitched on the Table-board, and then vanished away. Upon this the Examinant, and the other two persons looking again in *Styles* Poll, found it very red and like raw Beef . . . The Examinant demanding . . . what the Fly was, she confessed it was her Familiar, and that she felt it tickle in her Poll, and that was the usual time when her Familiar came to her.[23]

It is not just devils who can come and go in the form of flies. The Norse god Loki, associated with fire, air and deceit, changes himself into a fly to enter the chamber of Freyja and steal her necklace.[24] Offenbach's *Orpheus in the Underworld* includes a scene in which Jupiter looks at the keyhole of Eurydice's boudoir in the underworld and thinks 'Something exquisitely small to get through that exquisite keyhole, and something at the same time enchantingly seductive. I have it! A fly! A golden Godfly!'[25] His buzzing song and beautiful gilded wings complete the seduction.

The powers of the fly to breed almost anywhere are suggested by an early eighteenth-century account of a Monsieur Oufle, who was beset by delusions of spirits and devils, his obsession being fuelled by the extensive library of magical and occult books he had imprudently amassed. Rising early one morning to mug up on measures to avoid being besieged by spectres and phantoms, '[h]e was unlucky in what he first read; for he found what he did not search for, I wou'd say, the Art of making frightful Spectres appear, by a Man's Head, by Putrefaction turn'd into Flies, and then into Dragons'.[26] Our narrator's footnote solemnly refers us to the suggestions of Albertus Magnus on the relations between flies and dragons: 'The Ancients say, That the hinder part of the Head is its first and principal part; that it forms Worms in a little time after the Death of a Man, that in seven Days they become Flies, and that in fourteen, they change to Dragons, whose biting is instantly mortal.'[27]

This must indeed have been a turn-up for the books for the poor beleaguered Monsieur Oufle, who had a particular dread of flies, believing them to be a favourite form for devils to assume:

he affirm'd also, that the Devil frequently appear'd in the Shape of those Insects; for which Reason, he wou'd not suffer any Fruit on the Table, for fear it shou'd draw them thither. A certain Person having shew'd him one in a Microscope, when he saw its Horns, its Trunk, its purple Eyes, its hairy Legs, its cloven Feet, and in short, its whole Body together, representing a Figure which to him seem'd so much the more hideous, because he never believ'd 'twas what he saw it to be; he thought it a very proper Habitation for the Devil. He had the same Opinion of Butterflies, to the great Misfortune of all those who came within his reach; for he never spar'd one of them.[28]

The most important link between flies and devils is supplied by the figure of Beelzebub, Satan's lieutenant, whose name is believed to mean 'lord of the flies' – indeed, Satan himself is sometimes thus styled. The term Beelzebub appears in the Old Testament as the name of the god of the Philistine city of Ekron, whom Ahaziah sought to consult about the prospects of his recovery after a fall. As touchy as ever about rival divinities, the Lord intercepted his messengers and sent them back to tell him not to book any more dancing lessons as, no, he was not going to recover. Beelzebub is *Ba'al-z^ebub*, the lord of the flies. It has been surmised that this local god got his name from the fact that he offered protection against flies, or the maladies they conveyed, and is thus equivalent to the Greek *apomuios* and the Roman God Myiagrus – the 'fly-chaser'. The name does not appear elsewhere in the Old Testament, but apparently reappears in the New Testament, modified, in most manuscripts, to Beelzeboul (Matthew 12. 24; Luke 11. 15), when Christ is accused of

Beelzebub in Collin de Plancy's *Dictionnaire infernale* (1863).

Beelzebub explained, in a passage from Gabriel Naudaeus's *History of Magick . . .* (1657).

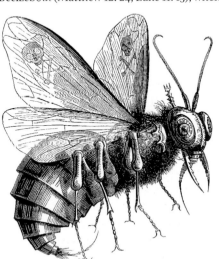

❝ *The History of* MAGICK.

all other exorbitancies and iniquities, which in time so far prevailed over vertue, that God could do no lesse than send an universall Deluge to cleanse the earth from all those abominations. But the waters were no sooner return'd into their place, but this spirit of presumption, this *Beelzebub*, Prince of Flies, began to renew his practices, and to lay the foundation of his second Monarchy in those weak minds, which are most easily taken, and entangled in the cobwebs of a multitude of suspicious operations, strange sacrifices, and magicall superstitions. It is not indeed possible to particularize and tell justly, who, of all the men of this second age of the world, was the first instrument of this fatall enemy of Nature, to disperse his conjurations over the habitable earth, as we find them now received and practised.

using the power of a powerful devil to cure those possessed of evil spirits. It is not clear quite what the name of this powerful entity signifies. It could mean *Ba'al-z^ebul*, 'lord of the house'. Another suggestion is that the term is founded on the Ugaritic word *zbl*, meaning prince – in which case Beelzebul would mean the 'lord of princes'.[29] If Beelzebul is indeed a modification of Beelzebub, this seems to represent a considerable promotion for a minor local deity. Of course, it is quite possible that this Beelzebul is a different god altogether. Others detect in the name the influence of the Aramaic word *zebel*, meaning dung or excrement, which is an obvious development from Beelzebub, if not a deliberate, disrespectful smearing of it.[30] Other modifications are found in magical and popular literature – Beelzebut, on the model of other demons and deities with names ending in -ut or -uth, and Beelzebud.[31] Beelzebul is named as the prince of demons in the *Testament of Solomon*, a magical text from between the first and third centuries AD.[32] This derivation is scarcely enough on its own to account for all the stories of devils or the devil appearing in the guise of flies, but it must have exerted a considerable influence.

Christ with the Devil: Beelzebub is associated, by contiguity at least, with his emblematic fly in this page from the *Isabella Breviary*.

If the mark of the devil is his capacity to command the flies that are his familiars and accomplices, then the exalted status of more august beings is also evidenced in the power that they exercise over flies, though on the grounds of their antagonism rather than affinity. There are many stories of the efficacy of sacrifice in persuading the gods or the flies themselves directly to ensure fly-free festivities. Pliny writes that the people of Elis 'invoke the god Myiacores when a swarm of flies brings plague, the flies dying as soon as a sacrifice to this god has been performed'.[33] Sometimes fly-catching or prevention is seen as an aspect of a god, such as Zeus or Apollo. According to Pausanias, the people of Elis offered sacrifices to Zeus in his aspect as the averter of flies.[34] Sometimes the desire to be free of flies precipitated the figure of a special god known as 'Myagros', the fly-chaser.

The demonic associations of flies made them apt to signify sin and vice in general. In AD 385 St Jerome wrote a letter to a woman called Marcella, thanking her for a number of gifts she had sent to women of his community, including sackcloth, chairs, tapers and fly-flaps, and commenting on their symbolic appropriateness: 'when you offer to matrons little fly-flaps to brush away mosquitoes, it is a charming way of hinting that they should at once check voluptuous feelings, for "dying flies," we are told, "spoil sweet ointment."'[35]

Flies have general significations of evil or vice in other religious traditions. In *The Questions of King Milinda*, a Buddhist text dealing with the conversion of King Menander (Milinda), who ruled in the area known as modern Afghanistan from 115 to 90 BC, the spider is represented as a symbol of spiritual precaution:

> Just, O king, as the road spider weaves the curtain of its net
> on the road, and whatsoever is caught therein, whether

worm, or fly, or beetle, that does he catch and eat; just so, O king, should the strenuous Bhikshu, earnest in effort, spread the curtain of the net of self-possession over the six doors (of his six senses), and if any of the flies of evil are caught therein, there should he seize them. This, O king, is the quality of the road spider he ought to have.[36]

An early – and anatomically inaccurate – spider pursues a fly, in John Payne's *Animalium quadrupedum avium florum* (1625).

As well as being emissaries or symbols of evil, flies are also sometimes accorded considerable demonic power. A seventeenth-century text about Lapp and Finnish culture describes how Finnish wizards use demonic flies to effect their injurious purposes:

an Inhabitant of *Helieland*, who is still alive, going towards the mountains in *Norway* to hunt Bears, came to a cave under the side of a hill, where he found an image rudely shapen, which was the Idoll of some *Finlander*; near this stood a *Ganeska*, or magical satchel: he opened this, and found in it several blewish flies crawling about, which they call *Gans*, or Spirits, and are daily sent out by the *Finlanders* to execute their devilish designs. But he seems to intimate no more by this word *Gan*, then that very thing that endangers mens health, and lives. For he saies that these *Finlanders* cannot live peacably, except they let out of their *Ganeska* or *Gankiid*, which is the satchel, every day one of the *Gans*, that is a fly or devil.[37]

One of the most developed and explicit fly-demons is described in the laws of purification in the *Vendidad*, a compilation of religious laws and mythical tales forming part of the *Zend-Avesta* (of *c.* AD 330) the sacred book of the Parsis, followers of Mazdeism or Zoroastrianism. Here, the impurity that enters the body at death is described as a fly-demon. The book contains a series of Fargards, or questions put to the divine spirit Ahura by the mortal Zarathustra. In Fargard VII we read:

Ahura Mazda answered: 'Directly after death, as soon as the soul has left the body, O Spitama Zarathustra! The Drug Nasu comes and rushes upon him, from the regions of the north, in the shape of a raging fly, with knees and tail sticking out, all stained with stains, and like unto the foulest Khrafstras.'[38]

The *Vendidad* also describes an elaborate process for washing away the defilement that comes from touching a corpse. As one washes one portion, the Drug Nasu rushes to another: from forehead, to jaws, right and left ear, right and left shoulder, all the way down to the feet, whence the demon is finally driven out.[39]

Not surprisingly, flies have often been subject to ecclesiastical condemnation, with the power to dispel flies being a proof of sanctity. When St Bernard of Clairvaux was preaching in a church of Foigny around 1121, his congregation was badly discomposed by a swarm of flies. St Bernard pronounced an anathema on the miscreant *Muscidae*, upon which they all expired, in such numbers that monks needed shovels to remove them.[40] The belief in the efficacy of ecclesiastical process survived well into the medieval period and beyond.[41] While there was an undoubted tendency to think of insects and other vermin as diabolical in nature as well as effect, ecclesiastical authorities could also be charmingly and ludicrously scrupulous about giving the creatures concerned the chance to answer the charges against them.

If the Church has usually set its face against flies, there are also examples of their recruitment in the struggle against the

The 'plague of flies' from Exodus 8 makes up scene four from *The Ten Plagues of Egypt* in this undated German engraving.

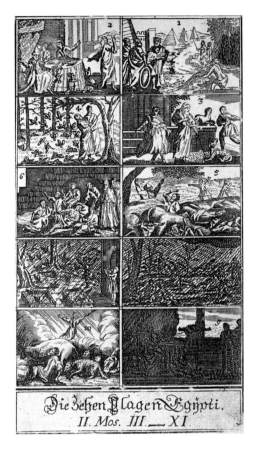

Die Zehen Plagen Egypti.
II. Mos. III.___XI.

enemies of faith, encouraged no doubt by the story of the plague of flies that descended on the Egyptians in Exodus. In AD 350, at the end of a long siege by the Persian king, Sapor II, of the Roman town of Nisibis in Mesopotamia, St James, the bishop of the town, stood on the walls and prayed that the Persians be afflicted with the same plague as the Egyptians. At once, a huge swarm of flies fell upon the besiegers, driving the men and their animals to a frenzy, and causing their precipitate withdrawal, stung and pestered.[42] Flies were also drafted in to repel French invaders of the Catalan town of Girona. It is said that when, in 1285, the invaders tore open the tomb of St Narcissus, one of the town's patron saints, who was martyred in 307 and is buried in the cathedral, a swarm of flies flew out and drove them away. The salvation of Girona is commemorated to this day by the chocolate flies that are a speciality of local bakers. Salvador Dalí, for whom flies had an enduring fascination and who was brought up a few miles away in Figueres, recalled the event in a small bronze sculpture entitled *St Narcissus of the Flies*, which features a fly on the stomach of the bishop.

Flies do not invariably have negative associations. One of the earliest ethnographic accounts of the people of Southern Africa reported that the Hottentots worship as a 'benign Deity' a fly-like insect 'of the Dimensions of a Child's little Finger; the Back green; the Belly speck'd with White and Red . . . provided with Two Wings, and on its Head with Two Horns', which is said to be unique to their country.

The name of the fly *Musca hottentota* seems to derive from its large abdomen, probably with an allusion to the large posterior of the South African 'Hottentot Venus' (Sara Baartman) who was exhibited in Europe from 1810 to 1814. This illustration comes from Edward Donovan's contemporary *Natural History of British Insects* (1803–13).

To this little winged Deity, when ever they set Sight upon it, they render the highest Tokens of Veneration. And if it honours, forsooth, a *Kraal* with a Visit, the Inhabitants assemble about it in Transports of Devotion, as if the Lord of the Universe was come among 'em . . . 'tis impossible to drive out of a *Hottentot*'s Head, that the Arrival of this Insect in a *Kraal*, brings Grace and Prosperity to all the Inhabitants. They believe, that all their Offences to that Moment are buried in Oblivion, and all their Iniquities done away . . . If this Insect happens to alight upon a Hottentot, he is look'd upon as a Man without Guilt, and distinguish'd and reverenc'd as a Saint and the Delight of the Deity ever after.[43]

The account goes on to explain the ritual attached to the honouring of the one so touched by divinity, which calls for an

The Hottentots worshipping a fly, from Peter Kolb, *The Present State of the Cape of Good-Hope; or, a Particular Account of the Several Nations of the Hottentots . . .* (1731).

The Hottentots adore a certain Infect.

ox to be sacrificed and the animal's fat and caul to be twisted into a kind of rope, which stinking garland the chosen one must wear collarwise round his neck until it rots off, thereby, one imagines, ensuring continuing divine visitations.

The fly's acute responsiveness to light has associated it with the worship of the sun. An early commentator reported that flies were among the creatures sacrificed to the sun by the ancient Peruvians.[44] The solar associations of the fly motivate Kenneth Patchen's angry poem, in which a fly declares

You peculiar pink stinks been crowdin'
On the Sun's Life   Look out!
Green Him's home's the last place
You should mess with   Move it![45]

Perhaps the greatest theological dignity accorded to the fly is to be found in the Babylonian epic of Gilgamesh, dating from about 2000 BC, which contains a flood narrative that parallels the narrative of the flood in Genesis. In Tablet XI of the Gilgamesh narrative, the flood is brought about by a consortium of the gods, led by Anu and his counsellor Enlil. Where the Lord himself repents his decision to destroy man in the Old Testament narrative, there is discord among the gods in the Gilgamesh version, with Belet-ili, the goddess who has created man, bewailing the destruction, and the gods themselves taking fright. When Uta-napishti, whose role parallels that of Noah, comes to rest on a mountain, he makes a sacrifice of reed, cedar and myrtle:

The gods did smell the savour,
the gods did smell the savour sweet,
the gods gathered like flies around the man making sacrifice.[46]

That this comparison is not meant to be disparaging is suggested by the fact that flies feature as a symbol of fertility and trust when Belet-ili joins the sacrifice. First of all the gods are drawn like flies by the sweet aroma and then the symbolic flies on Belet-ili's necklace act to restore the covenant between her and Anu, the father of the gods, and also to reaffirm the continuity between gods and men.

> Then at once Belet-ili arrived,
> she lifted the flies of lapis lazuli that Anu had made for
>   their courtship:
> 'Oh gods let these great beads in this necklace of mine
>   make me remember these days, and never forget
>   them!'[47]

In the Genesis narrative (assuming it to be derived from the Gilgamesh epic, or from a common source), the various gods have coalesced into the one God, and the discord of the gods in the Gilgamesh narrative has been rationalized into the Lord's change of mind about destroying his people. It may be far beneath the dignity of the Lord God to be, like his Babylonian predecessors, a Lord of flies, but his fly-like susceptibility to aroma is still marked, for it seems to be just this that prompts his softening towards his creation, just as it draws the gods in the Gilgamesh epic: 'And the LORD smelled the sweet savour; and the LORD said in his heart, I will not again curse the ground any more for man's sake' (Genesis 8. 21). Since we must assume that the creative power of Belet-ili has also been subsumed into the person of the Lord, there is no sign of her necklace of flies: unless, that is, the renewed covenant between Belet-ili and Anu signified by the linked flies has its counterpart in the radiant token the Lord places in the sky, as a recurring reminder of

An implausibly
lapis-lazuli-coloured
fly, from Donovan's
*Natural History of
British Insects.*

his covenant with his people: 'I do set my bow in the cloud, and it shall be for a token of a covenant between me and the earth' (Genesis 9. 13).

3 Sticky Fun

More than any other creature, the fly has a reputation for hedonism. As a consequence, attitudes towards the fly take the print of prevailing attitudes towards physical pleasure. The fly takes its pleasure promiscuously, restlessly, unswervably, unashamedly. Its inordinate love of sweetness is a powerful expression of this love of pleasure. In his great poem of universal blessing, *Jubilate Agno*, Christopher Smart celebrated the fly 'whose health is the honey of the air', adding however, 'but he feeds on the thing strangled, and perisheth'.[1] Vincent Dethier, who devoted a lifetime to the study of fly behaviour and built an entire book around the question of the fly's hunger and the patterns of behaviour it impels, points to a few surprising facts about the fly's appetite for sugar. First of all, it is highly sensitive. A fly can detect sugar in water at concentrations far weaker than a human being can. It is also discriminating; flies detect the sweetness of different kinds of sugars – grape sugar, cane sugar, malt sugar and others – in the same ratio of sensitivity as human beings. The fly's quest for sweetness is assisted by the fact that it has organs of taste in its feet. When a fly's foot encounters something sweet, it produces as a reflex the lowering of the proboscis to siphon up whatever goodness lies beneath. Dethier proposes the following elegant, if unfeeling, method for proving this reflex. A fly that has been anaesthetized by being

Fly extending its proboscis to feed on an apple.

put in the freezer compartment for a few minutes is glued feet upwards to a pencil. Lowered over a saucer of water, the fly – which will very likely be thirsty, for, partly as a result of the large ratio of their surface area to their mass, leading to high rates of evaporation, flies nearly always are – will lower its proboscis to drink as soon as its feet touch the surface of the water, and then retract the proboscis when its thirst has been slaked. The purpose of this preliminary exercise is to make sure that one can distinguish between thirst and hunger in the fly. If the fly is then lowered over a saucer of sugared water, it will lower its proboscis to suck again. Dipping its feet back in the unsweetened water will cause the proboscis to be raised, and so on, as many times as one cares to move the fly between feeding stations; each time the feet detect sugar in the water, the proboscis will come down; when no sugar is evident to its tasting feet, then it will not.[2] Thus, the fly's habit of trampling across its food is purposive and investigative rather than slovenly.

A house fly proboscis, from Samuelson and Braxton-Hicks, *Humble Creatures: The Earthworm and the Common Housefly . . .* (1858).

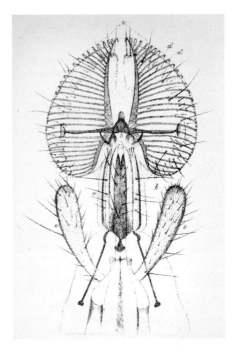

Houseflies will commonly exude a drop, or, as here, a bubble of digestive fluid to liquefy their food.

Although both male and female flies are drawn to sweetness, female flies of most species of Diptera who are preparing for egg laying are more likely than males to look for protein, which they may derive from decaying organic matter or animal excretions. Male flies not only do not require protein to build bodily mass (for, once hatched, flies do not grow), but are much more active than female flies, for which activity sugars provide a fast energy source: one estimate found that male house flies spent about 24.3 per cent of their time in motion, and 27.9 per cent of their time resting, while for female house flies the proportions were 12.7 per cent and 40.6 per cent.[3] So the flies that cluster around a jam doughnut are likely to be male, while the flies that crawl around the milky lips or brimming eyes of babies are likely to be female.

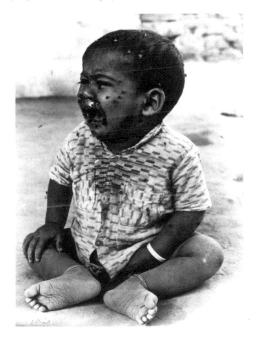

Babies like this one covered in flies have become emblematic of poverty and illness in Third World countries. The flies are likely to be in search of protein and thus female.

The attraction of flies to sweet sticky substances that can ensnare them means that they are often used to dramatize the perils attaching to pleasure – as in this cigarette card illustrating *Aesop's Fables*, c. 1921.

The appetite for sweetness has often made flies the vehicles of warnings against the pursuit of pleasure for its own sake. Flies are popularly imagined getting trapped or stuck, sometimes by the effect of their own appetites, as for example in Thomas Blague's little moral fable of gluttony in his *Schole of Wise Conceytes* (1569): 'Flies flew into a holeful of honie, wherof they did eate: their feete stucke fast therein, that they coulde not escape, who being nigh choaked, sayde: Ah wretches, which for a little meate doe perishe.'[4] Francis Quarles warns of the traps lying in wait for the pleasure-seeker:

> The Sun-delighting Flye repayres, at first,
> To the full Cup, only to quench her thirst;
> But, oftentimes, she sports about the Brinke,
> And sipps so long till she be drownd in drinke:
> When wanton leysure shall present thine eye
> With lavish Cups, Remember but the Flye.[5]

His son John recycled the trope, adding a warning about the spiritual death that a fly-like devotion to pleasure brings:

Martinus Nellius, *Still life with Rummer*, c. 1650, oil on wood.

Man (like a Fly) still buzzes up and down
From cup to cup, and sips on, till he drown
Himself in pleasure; tears no stander by:
And how can Heav'n love such a drunken Fly?[6]

A more extended treatment of this theme is found in a poem of around 1781 by George Keate, which tells of the arrival of two hungry flies during the dessert course at an elaborate dinner. During the enthusiastic toasts 'To *Liberty*, and *Church* and *King*', two flies 'extravagantly gay/The idle beings of a day' appear, drawn by the tempting aroma of the fruits, syrups and sweetmeats with which the board is spread.[7] Their desire for sweetness extends not only to every flower in the meadow, but also to the sweet-smelling persons of the young ladies. The sexual hints are not very deeply concealed:

> Nay, dar'd the fragrant odour seek
> Of Stella's lip, or Stella's cheek:
> Nor would one single wish restrain
> Their *Summum Bonum* to attain [p. 149].

The flies – 'Our young Adventurers' – seem fairly certain to be male, as they trample across the luscious fruit, sipping and piercing, 'with insatiate touch' (p. 150). Finally, and inevitably, one of them spies a jar of floating sweetmeats and 'letting ev'ry Passion loose,/He plung'd into the tempting juice' (p. 151).

Giovanna Garzoni, *Dish of Plums, Hazel-nuts and a Fly*, c. 1646–64, watercolour on parchment.

Thoſe Foolés *whom* Beauties *Flame doth bli nde,*
Feele Death, *where* Life *they thought to finde.*

40

An emblem
accompanying
George Wither's
poetic warning
against pleasure.
The motto around
the outside reads
'pleasure leads
to death as well
as life'.

The attraction of flies to light, and especially artificial flames, also suggested moral lessons. Pictures of flies singed in flames were a standard feature of emblem books, often accompanied by poetical warnings like this one from George Wither's collection of emblems of 1635:

When you doe next behold the wanton *Flyes*
About the shining *Candle*, come to play,
Untill the *Light* thereof hath dimm'd their Eyes,
Or, till the *Flame* hath sing'd their Wings away:
Remember, then, this *Emblem*; and, beware
You be not playing at such harmefull Games:
Consider, if there sit no *Female*, there,
That overwarmes you, with her *Beauties Flames*.
Take heed, you doe not over dally so
As to inflame the Tinder of *Desire*;
But, shun the Mischiefe, e're too late it grow,
Lest you be scorched in that *Foolish-Fire*.[8]

Ben Jonson's 'The Hour-Glass' beautifully imagines the 'small dust' running through the hour-glass as the remains of 'one that loved/And in his mistress' flame, playing like a fly,/Turned to cinders by her eye', unable even in death to find rest.[9] A poem by Joseph Mitchell of a century later that became a popular song conflated inundation and incineration. The fly drawn to the lady's eye is addressed grandiosely: 'Deluded Fly! that thus presum'd/T'invade celestial Light! . . . / You hop'd to mingle in a Flame,/And, Phoenix like, expire!'[10] But, drowning in the lady's tears, the fly is less like Phaethon, driving the runaway chariot of the sun-god, than like Icarus, whose fate, having flown too close to the sun, is to plummet into water: 'How vain was your ambitious Aim?/How strange to drown in Fire?'[11]

The fly's seeming devotion to pleasure has often been used to justify an allegorical contrast with bees, ants and other

The accompanying text to this emblem by Claude Paradin draws on the mistaken belief, deriving from Plutarch, that flies cannot cling to polished surfaces. Its lesson is that 'so it fareth with us when we are in prosperitie and have all things at will, we use quickly to fall into diverse and sundrie sinnes: whereas on the other side being touched sometimes with crosses and afflictions, we stay our selves in some measure.'

Labuntur nitidis, scabrisque
tenatius hærent.
Flies do fall downe from slipperie place, but
stick fast vpon the hard and rough.

social insects. Many cultures have a version of a story that explains how the differences arose between provident insects such as the bee, which creates sweetness and stores it up for the future, and the fly, which merely consumes it, heedless of the morrow. K. Langloh Piper collected from the Noongahburrah people of Australia a story of the Wurrunnunnah and the Bunnyyarl who at one time lived together and were not yet

Musca aurula (middle) and *Musca semi-argentata* (bottom), 'gilded flies' from Donovan's *Natural History of British Insects*.

distinguished from each other. The Wurrunnunnah counsel the Bunnyyarl to join them in laying in stores of nectar from the flowers as the winter is on its way, but the Bunnyyarl continue to hang idly around rubbish, reasoning that they can always share whatever the Wurrunnunnah have stockpiled. Tired of doing all the work, the Wurrunnunnah go off to live separately as bees, and the Bunnyyarl become flies.[12] Flies are consequently natural metaphors for social parasites, as in Shelley's 'Queen Mab', which contains the following protest against the idle ruling classes:

> Those gilded flies
> That, basking in the sunshine of a court,
> Fatten on its corruption! – what are they?
> – The drones of the community; they feed
> On the mechanic's labour.[13]

Shelley may have been imputing more than appetite for food to his aristocratic parasites. In its original context, the 'gilded fly' pops up in King Lear's vision of unrestricted universal copulation: 'The Wren goes to't, and the small gilded fly/Does lecher in my sight./Let copulation thrive' (*King Lear*, IV. 6)

This didactic structure often reappears in the entomological allegories produced for younger readers in the nineteenth century. One of these is *Changed to a Fly*, a book by the Polish writer Zofia Urbanowska, which was translated into French in 1895. The story concerns a little boy called Gustave who is full of promises and good resolutions, but lacking in all concentration and constancy. On the day of his birthday, Gustave's grandfather gives him a watch and assigns him a tutor. The horrified boy imprudently proclaims that he would rather be a fly, at which point a fairy arrives, and effects the mooted transformation,

The readers of Samuelson's and Braxton-Hicks's *Humble Creatures: The Earthworm and the Housefly* seem to be invited by this frontispiece to appreciate the dignity and worth of this negligible-seeming creature in the order of things.

promising him: 'You will remain a fly until you learn to love work and deserve to be called a man.'[14] Gustave's reduced size and magnified eyes allow him to learn a number of lessons about striving and useful toil from the examples of the animals he meets – a sparrow, a spider, some beetles, some earthworms.

However, the story has to be skewed somewhat to enable this understanding to come about. For, far from being changed into a fly, as the title of the story would suggest, it is clear that, as the fluttering, inconstant being he is at the beginning of the story, he already is to all intents and purposes a fly. It is the condition of the fly that embodies his all too human frailty and lack of purpose. He is given the fly's smallness and optical power, but none of its other characteristics, which he must leave behind in order to regain his human shape. He is, in fact, changed from, rather

than into, a fly. The optics he brings to bear on the natural world are governed by the values of work, duty, utility, self-sacrifice.

The fly's appetite is as promiscuous as it is intense, encompassing as it does both sewage and sweetness, and thus seems to bring the two opposite principles into equivalence. Among a host of other extravagant fantasies about the relations between men and animals, James W. Redfield's *Comparative Physiognomy* (1852) proposed a kind of moral taxonomy based upon the degrees of fermentation undergone by an animal's staple foods, believing that 'each stage of fermentation, as to the appetite that demands it, is a stage in the down-hill course of deception and mockery, of

The fly's susceptibility to pleasure is often suggested as a weakness for alcoholic beverages, as in this painting by Georg Flegel (*Still-life with Carafe of Wine*, 1637, oil on wood).

cowardice, cruelty, and degradation'.[15] Earlier in his book, he had also proclaimed that 'the appetite for substances in a state of decomposition is promoted by cowardice' (p. 105). Thus he could distinguish between animals who feed on nectar and the honey that bees make from it and animals who crave sugar.

All animals that live on honey, or are very fond of it, are remarkable for courage, and also for carefulness, which is another name for caution, as, for example, the bee, the humming-bird, and the bear; but animals that are in the way of eating sugar instead of honey, and seem to prefer it, are deficient in those qualities, as, for example, the house-fly, the ant that lives in the sugar-bowl, and not infrequently the wasp, besides which we may mention children that live on cakes and confectionery, and people who are very fond of sweetmeats and preserves [p. 270].

Inebriation and putrefaction go together for Redfield, being instanced in the fondness of the French for both wine and ripe game, as well as in the drunken Irishman. Encouraged in his speculations perhaps by the word 'bar-fly', he warns that '[t]he drunkard on his last legs may be compared to the blow fly when it has come to the degree of perfection in the fondness for carrion' (p. 278). Following the groggy logic that makes the fly responsible for producing the putrefaction upon which it depends, Redfield says that the drunken man inhabits a kind of mephitic nimbus of delirium, formed by his own foul emanations:

The inebriate lives in the very atmosphere that engenders suspicion – the putridity of his own breath – in which the blow-fly, the crow, and the hog, with all their cowardly apprehensions, might be deluded into the idea of safety, as in the presence of something dead [p. 108].

Some of these associations seem to be reactivated in the no-nonsense 'open-source' beer marketed in Australia as Blowfly Beer by the Brewtopia beer company.[16] Recent research has suggested not only that the weakness for alcohol may be more generalized among animals than we might suspect but also that there may be a particular link between humans and flies in this respect.

The evolutionary biologist Robert Dudley has suggested that the attractiveness of sweet, ripe fruits to yeasts, which produce ethanol among their by-products, made olfactory sensitivity to ethanol a useful evolutionary advantage.[17] There might be good reason for fruit-flies and humans to share this sensitivity and predisposition. Thus it is not surprising that researchers interested in the genetics of addiction should look to the fruit-fly for insights. Flies and humans show very similar responses to alcohol, including stimulation at low doses, contrasting with sedation at higher doses. The blood–alcohol concentration required to make human beings and fruit-flies inebriated is closely comparable – between 0.1 and 0.2 per cent. It is hoped that mutant genes may be found in *Drosophila* that may identify a genetic component in the susceptibility to alcoholism in humans.[18]

As we have seen, sweetness and sexuality are commonly associated, which may explain the fact that flies have a reputation for sexual as well as gastronomic indulgence. Aristotle observes the difficulty of pulling copulating flies apart: 'these creatures are, under the circumstances, averse to separation; for the intercourse of the sexes in their case is of long duration, as may be observed with common everyday insects, such as the fly and the cantharis'.[19] The intensity and lengthiness of flies' copulation are also remarked upon in Lucian's encomium, in which he writes that '[t]he male is not on and off again in a moment, like the cock; he covers the female a long time'.[20] It has also often been reported that flies couple on the wing. Mating Australian bush flies will stay joined for an average of 1 hour 20 minutes if they are undisturbed.[21] The sexual reputation of flies lies behind the disgusted characterization that Wordsworth offered Ralph Waldo Emerson of a novel of which he disapproved: 'He proceeded to abuse Goethe's Wilhelm Meister heartily. It was full of all manner of fornication. It was

Some flies have a fondness for the sweet nectar of flowers, as this 1740s illustration by August Johann Roesel von Rosenhof indicates.

like the crossing of flies in the air. He had never gone farther than the first part; so disgusted was he that he threw the book across the room.'[22] Maupassant's story 'Mouche' draws on the lubricious reputation of the fly in its characterization of a pretty, prattling, promiscuous young girl, who sleeps with all five members of a rowing crew. Her undeluded lover, N'a-qu'un-Oeil (Monocle), growls that she has got her name 'Because she settles on all kinds of carrion'.[23]

The reputation that flies have for sexual athleticism may also derive in part from the fabled aphrodisiac properties of the substance known as Spanish Fly. This really has nothing to do with flies at all, since it derives from the ground-up bodies of an emerald-green beetle known as *Lytta vesicatoria* (or sometimes *Cantharis vesicatoria*), which has the popular name of the blister-beetle, on account of the intense burning sting its secretions impart to sensitive membranes. It is these properties that led to the crushed cantharides being used as a diuretic and the irritant, itching effects of the substance on the genito-urinary tract may have given it its reputation for inflaming or invigorating sexual desire. The sweets that were used to disguise the horrible taste of the cantharadin were known as *pastilles de Richelieu*, after the Duc de Richelieu, who used to give them to his mistresses. The Marquis de Sade was brought to trial in 1772 after nearly killing two women to whom he had administered the

The single-mindedness of flies engaged in copulation has often been remarked on.

poison in aniseed sweets (the aniseed was not just to render the toxin more palatable, it was also to increase the girls' flatulence, so they could fart to order into the Marquis's mouth).[24]

Another reason that the fly has been regarded as the embodiment of amoral hedonism or licentiousness is its prodigious capacity for breeding. In his book of 1913 warning against flies, Edward Halford Ross narrates the life of a female fly, in order to emphasize her dangerous fecundity, though her femaleness also adds a sting to the irresponsibility of a life spent in the pursuit of various forms of 'sticky fun':

> This day was full of adventure. She met a male fly and mated with him; her consort thereupon deserted her . . . She galumphed with delight at her freedom, for the tide of her life was at flood . . . hers was the life of pleasure . . . what matter the germs of death – they were but sticky fun to her.[25]

Another positive aspect of the sluttishness of flies is their capacity to suggest resurrection. Pliny's belief that drowned flies were capable of being resuscitated by heat survived well into the seventeenth century. Robert Boyle seriously wondered whether flies really died in the winter, or were not 'rather Benumm'd than Dead, because regularly recovering the manifest actions of life in the Spring, (nor oftentimes before, if a due application of heat be made unto them'.[26] Unfortunately, his own experiments with restoring the breath of life to flies that had been asphyxiated in his vacuum chamber did not give much encouragement to this theory.

In fact, the stories about the powers of flies to survive extremity or revive after death have more foundation than one might expect. In 1899 the Canadian entomologist D. W.

Coquillet reported his discovery of a fly the eggs and larvae of which develop in the pools of crude oil that bubbled up from the ground in California. He named it *Psilopa petroliti*, or the 'petrol fly'. Its fondness for the black stuff is all the more remarkable, given the recognition since ancient times of the aversion of flies to oils of all kind. The fabled capacity of flies to revive after being subjected to apparently lethal stress also finds confirmation in the case of a Nigerian fly known as *Polypedilium vanderplanki*, the larvae of which develop in pools of water in granite rocks, which are subject to evaporation several times a day. The larvae can survive for eight or ten years in a state of desiccated 'cryptobiosis', or suspended animation, until immersion in water restores them to full function.[27]

Flies provide more than mere analogies for human pleasure. That flies can not only exemplify but provoke sexual feeling is wryly confirmed in Fleur Adcock's little poem 'Coupling':

On the wall above the bedside lamp
a large crane-fly is jump-starting
a smaller crane-fly – or vice versa.
They do it tail to tail, like Volkswagens:
their engines must be in their rears.

It looks easy enough. Let's try it.[28]

Like the crane flies evoked by Fleur Adcock, some hover flies, such as this pair of *Spaerophoria scripta*, mate with joined abdomens.

The literal nature of Christ's resurrection is proved by the attendant fly in Giovanni Santi's *Christ in the Tomb* (*c.* 1490, oil and tempera on wood).

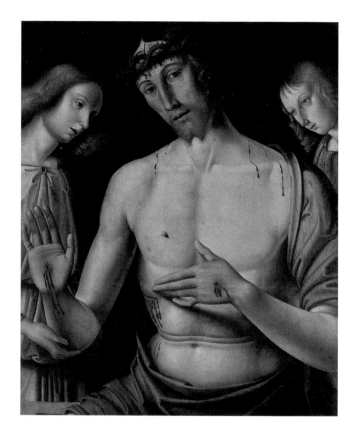

Flies can also participate in human sexual pleasure, by acting as relays or intermediaries. The Greek poet Meleager wrote a pair of poems, in the first of which he calls mosquitoes away from their feasting on the body of his lover, threatening them with 'the strength of my jealous hands', and in the second of which he sends out a mosquito to remind his lover of his devotion:

The fly that crawls titillatingly across the alabaster flesh of this lady is both a surrogate for the viewer's touch and suggests her own tolerant pleasure in that touch (Frans van der Myn, *The Fly*, 1742, oil on canvas).

Fly to her, swiftly fly, Mosquito, bearing my greeting:
Perch on the tip of her ear, and whisper it to her:
Say, He lies waking, longing for you: and you, sleeping.
Sleeping, O shameless girl!, have never a thought for who
loves you!

Buzz!
Chirr!
Off to her, sweetest Musician![29]

Flies are sexual mediators in Shakespeare's *Romeo and Juliet*. When Romeo receives word that he is to be banished from Verona, the agony of his exile from Juliet prompts in him a fevered, jealous image of the delicious liberties that even flies are allowed with 'the white wonder of dear Juliet's hand' but are forbidden to him: 'more courtship lives/In carrion-flies than Romeo' (*Romeo and Juliet*, III. iii, 39–41). Leopold Bloom's sexual-gastronomic reveries in Joyce's *Ulysses* are brought to a focus by the sight of two flies: 'Stuck on the pane two flies buzzed, stuck'.[30] We do not know if the flies are stuck because there is some sweet substance smeared there, or because they are clamped together in copulation.

Sexuality and horror are given a tactile or tactual imaging in Georges Bataille's *The Story of the Eye*. As Roland Barthes wrote in his essay of 1963 on it, the narrative is simply a flow of matter, eggs, eyes, tears, sperm, urine.[31] The climax comes in the final chapter, 'The Legs of the Fly', which sees the sexual murder of a priest, Don Aminado, by garrotting, an act performed by the narrator and his sexually voracious companions, Simone and Sir Edmund (as usual, it seems, no perversity can be taken seriously unless an English aristocrat is on the scene). After the murder of the priest, the serenely mechanical frenzies of forcible transmission and emission suddenly come to a halt in an image of blended disgust and fascination:

> [Simone] straddled the naked cadaver again, scrutinizing the purplish face with the keenest interest, she even sponged the sweat off the forehead and obstinately waved away a fly buzzing in a sunbeam and endlessly flitting back to alight on the face. All at once, Simone uttered a soft cry. Something bizarre and quite baffling had happened: this time, the insect had perched on the

corpse's eye and was agitating its long nightmarish legs on the strange orb. The girl took her head in her hands and shook it, trembling, then she seemed to plunge into an abyss of reflections.[34]

The fly is often taken as the uncomplicated embodiment of the pleasure principle, or the dream that pleasure might be as uncomplicated as we are confident it is for the fly. The elementariness of the fly's pleasure seems to prevent humans from forming any image or understanding of the possibility that it might suffer. How is it that we can imagine the fly so joyously alive in the pleasure of existence and yet so ontologically nugatory when it comes to the capacity for pain? It is as though the very negligibility of the fly's being makes it easy to imagine it being inundated by its pleasures, because we think of pleasure as coming upon us from outside sources; while the same negligibility makes it impossible to imagine the fly's suffering, since, we imagine, the capacity for pain is endogenous (suffering requires and confers a certain grandeur) and thus not to be attributed to a creature of such puny substance and brief persistence. Or perhaps it is that the magnification of sympathy required to acknowledge that flies might be capable of suffering, and the horror of the tortures and exterminations so gratuitously practised upon them through human history, must necessarily produce an intolerable overload of our sensibilities. We will see in the next chapter that this is the kind of anomaly and maladjustment of scale that the fly often provokes.

4 Orders of Magnitude

William Kirby, the most influential entomologist of the nineteenth century, began the first edition of his *Introduction to Entomology* with the protest that

> [I]n the minds of most men, the learned as well as the vulgar, the idea of the trifling nature of his [the entomologist's] pursuit is so strongly associated with that of the diminutive size of its objects, that an Entomologist (between whom and a Butterfly-hunter they seem unable to perceive any distinction) is synonymous with everything futile and childish.[1]

Alexander Pope found in entomology, and the preoccupation with flies in particular, an image for the trivial pedantries he saw ruling the day. In his *Dunciad* (1743) he had his Goddess of Dullness articulate the wish that the 'minute philosophers' who buzz around her should absorb themselves in small and insignificant things

> O! would the Sons of Men once think their Eyes
> And Reason giv'n them but to study *Flies*!
> See Nature in some partial narrow shape,
> And let the Author of the Whole escape.[2]

Though seemingly insignificant, the fly has often been imagined as the witness of momentous events: 'I', said the Fly, 'with my little eye'.

The interest in flies was again one of the characteristics of the 'solemn trifler' enumerated by William Cowper:

> whatever he discuss,
> Whether the space between the stars and us,
> Whether he measure earth, compute the sea,
> Weigh sunbeams, carve a fly, or spit a flea,
> The solemn trifler with his boasted skill
> Toils much, and is a solemn trifler still.[3]

And yet, as the considerations of pain and pleasure in the last chapter suggested, flies also have a reputation for being able to upset the natural hierarchies of size and importance in creation.

At the beginning of the earliest work of systematic entomology in Europe, Ulisse Aldrovandi justified his enterprise by observing that '[t]he Lion surpasses all animals, in strength, spirit and body, but the tiniest midge in Mesopotamia subdues it'.[4] Nineteenth-century entomologists were fond of repeating the assertion that the larvae of three blow flies (*Calliphora vomitoria*) would devour the carcass of a horse as quickly as a lion.

The microscope was the single most important influence in transforming the deprecation of what were thought to be imperfect and accidental creatures into confirmations of the extent and orderliness of divine design. Many early observers through the microscope reported their amazed delight at the intricacy and regularity to be found in creatures too tiny to be seen with the

This disproportionate conjuncture of a fly and a lynx, from a 1620s zoological compendium, reflects the popular coupling of large and small.

naked eye. Henry Baker had a particular fondness for flies, the beauty and variety of which make them even more fitted to connect the realms of the very small and the infinitely great:

> It would be endless to enumerate the different Sorts of *Flies*, which may continually be met with in the Meadows, Woods and Gardens; and impossible to describe their various Plumes and Decorations, surpassing all the Magnificence and Luxury of Dress in the Courts of the greatest Princes. Every curious Observer will find them out himself, and, with Amazement and Adoration, lift up his eyes from the *Creature* to the CREATOR.[5]

This bubble-blowing *Lucilia caesar* seems to add its comment to Seleucus' comparison of men to bubbles.

If the thought of the fly sometimes elevates the mind to thoughts of the Almighty, it can also be recruited to figure man's (sometimes rather grandiose) sense of his own cosmic insignificance. In his *Satyricon*, Petronius puts into the mouth of Seleucus, newly arrived from the funeral of his friend Chrysanthus, the reflection: 'how we bladders of wind strut about. We are meaner than flies: flies have their virtues, we are nothing but bubbles.'[6]

The volatility of scale and switch of perspective from the lower to the upper world are particularly marked in considerations of flies, partly because of the fascination provoked by the fly's eye. The compound eye of the fly is actually rather an ordinary affair, on the insect scale. The fly's eye consists only of 4,000 separate ommatidia, or light/dark sensors, compared to the dragonfly, which can have up to 30,000. These have also been called lenses, facets and, prettily, 'eye-pearls'.[7] But, perhaps because it is the most familiar and frequently seen of the insects, it is the fly's eye that is emblematic of the radically alien mode of entomological vision. Many writers have speculated about how and what a fly sees. Robert Hooke sets the tone for these accounts, when describing the apparent largeness of view of the fly:

> in each of these Hemispheres, I have been able to discover a Land-scape of those things which lay before my window, one thing of which was a large Tree, whose trunk and top I could plainly discover, as I could also the parts of my window, and my hand and fingers, if I held it between the Window and the Object.[8]

Hooke follows others in seeing the finger of the Almighty in the fashioning of the eye of the fly:

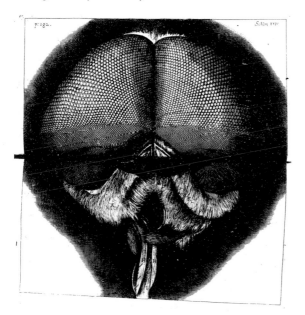

In his *Micrographia; or, Some Physiological Descriptions of Minute Bodies Made by Magnifying Glasses* of 1665, Robert Hooke was one of the first to appreciate and demonstrate the minute detail of the eye of a fly.

we need not doubt, but that there may be as much curiosity of contrivance and structure in every one of these Pearls, as in the eye of a Whale or Elephant, and the almighty's *Fiat* could as easily cause the existence of the one as the other; and as one day and a thousand years are the same with him, so may one eye and ten thousand.[9]

There may be a particularly curious effect of perspective inversion in the case of the fly, since not only do human beings see a great deal of flies, flies reciprocally see a great deal of us, and in our most intimate circumstances. Alberti refers to a story told by Pliny, Cicero, Strabo and others about the amazing powers of vision possessed by a particular lookout during the Punic wars, in order to draw a lesson about the even greater optical powers of the fly: 'If, as they say, a man, whose eyes occupy only a twentieth of the area of his head, could see from Piraeus the fleet issuing from the port of Carthage, what can the fly not

The head of a bluebottle.

ace, with its enormous eyes, what can escape its curiosity?'[10] The belief in the fly's superlative powers of vision probably lies behind the belief that flies provide useful medicine or prophylactics against eye complaints. Pliny reports that the Roman consul Mucianus carried a fly sewn into a linen pouch to protect him against eye diseases.[11] Galen's suggestion that flies beaten up with egg yolk to form a plaster are good for maladies of the eyes was still being repeated in the 1740s.[12] The fly's rapidity of flight and speed of reaction to movement make it easy to regard it as a living eye. And yet flies are also sometimes thought to be distinguished by restricted vision. Aristotle thought that the insect he knew as the *muops*, or the gadfly, died of dropsy in its eyes.[13] Pliny said the same thing of the *tabanus*, or stinging horsefly.[14] Richard Braithwaite affirms something similar of the gnat in 1634: 'Being bred in the marshes, hee is much subiect to rewmes and grievous defluxions of the eyes, and therefore cannot abide a smoakie roome.'[15] So actually Alberti may be teasing his readers with the common knowledge that in fact the fly's vision, though immensely acute, is in fact limited in range and detail. Indeed, the fly might actually be thought to be myopic rather than far-sighted (though it is tempting to believe that Aristotle's *muops* might have exerted an influence on the word myopia, the latter in fact has a different etymology). D'Arcy Wentworth Thompson, who, as well as being a biologist and mathematician, was also the translator of Aristotle's *History of Animals*, argued that there was a link between these beliefs in the blindness of flies and the game blindman's bluff, which is known in Greek as *muia kalke*, or The Brazen Fly. Thompson suggests that in the game '[t]he fly is the fierce and angry Gad-fly (*Tabanus*), whose incursion into a field sets the cattle wild with fear; and the one player is "the fly,"

A 'tufted gnat' in Robert Hooke's *Micrographia*.

Gnat and Tabanus from Thomas Moffett's *The Theater of Insects . . .* (1658).

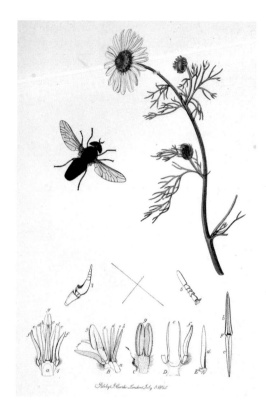

Tabinus alpinus, or the Alpine breeze fly, from John Curtis's 16-volume *British Entomology . . .* (1823–40).

and the rest are the cattle romping around', and provides as evidence of this tradition the fact that the fly named by Linneaus *Tabanus caecutiens* is called *blind knagg* in Sweden and *muia ceca* in Italy, where, he claims, the same phrase is used to name blindman's bluff.[16] The association between flies and imperfect sight is also evidenced in the name of the condition known as *muscae volitantes* (flying flies), caused by cell strands or fragments in the vitreous humour of the eye, in which the sufferer sees dancing spots or flecks.

The intensity of the scrutiny required to make out the detail of the fly's body, and of its eye, seems to be imaginatively returned in the cold and indifferent gaze it directs on us (not to mention the fact that flies are so attracted to eyes). Where the human eye requires magnification to see the fly, what it sees in the fly's eye is our miniaturization. When Fred Saxby set out his instructions on 'how to photograph through a fly's eye' in 1898 (in fact, his experiment used a cluster of lenses from a dragon fly's eye), he used as a focusing object a depiction of Queen Victoria, explaining: 'is it not appropriate that the noblest and greatest monarch the world has ever seen should be the subject

A house fly and a detail of a fly's eye, from Jacob Schaeffer's *Elementa Entomologica . . .* (1778).

of a photograph through the most infinitesimal lens known to science?'[17]

Ted Hughes's poem 'Fly Inspecta' effects a similar adjustment of perspective. The title summons up the ghost of the phrase 'fly specks', the most inconsiderable traces of the fly's presence. Hughes's poem seems itself to be just a series of wry jottings, but they are centred around the contrasting intensity of the fly's attention to its environment:

Fly
Is the Sanitary Inspector. He detects every speck
With his geiger counter.
Detects it, then inspects it
Through his multiple spectacles. You see him everywhere
Bent over his microscope.[18]

As with many of Hughes's poems, the actions evoked redouble the action of the poem itself. The fly's careful investigations mirror Hughes's, the poet 'bent over his microscope' to inspect the fly bent over his. The poem offers an exact mimicry of the fly's own careful accountancy:

He costs nothing, needs no special attention,
Just gets on with the job, totting up the dirt.

All he needs is a lick of sugar
Maybe a dab of meat –
Which is fuel for his apparatus.
We never miss what he asks for. He can manage
With so little you can't even tell
Whether he's taken it.[19]

The fly's redeeming attentions and accountings are the poem's own. The poem learns from its inspection of the fly at work the patience necessary to see it.

Like other insects, flies also seem to embody anomalies of quantity and number. Henry Baker called the animalcules revealed by his microscope 'those breathing Atoms, so small they are almost all Workmanship!'[20] There is in fact a significant etymological conversation between the words *atom* and *insect*. An atom, literally that which is without a cut, signifies something indivisible. The English word for insect comes from Latin *in-* and *secare*, to cut, which is a more or less literal rendering of Greek *entomos*, meaning with a cut in the middle or on the inside. The segmented bodies of insects seem to compromise their unity. Insects, which were often thought to be the smallest possible living creatures, mere motes of life, keep on providing evidence of the further divis-ibility of the elementary, all the way down, far beneath the threshold of visibility. The atom is always subject to more anatomy (literally, 'un-undividing'); there is always more divisibility in the visible. The insect is not only the one in the many, but also the many in the one. In reality, flies hover between the conditions of the singular and the plural. As Deleuze and Guattari observe, they are intrinsically multiple, like maggots and wolves:

> [W]e are not interested in characteristics; what interests us are modes of expansion, propagation, occupation, contagion, peopling. I am legion. The Wolf-Man fasci-nated by several wolves watching him. What would a lone wolf be? Or a whale, a louse, a rat, a fly? Beelzebub is the Devil, but the Devil as lord of the flies.[21]

Musca domestica   Tab. I.

Anatomizations of house flies, like this one from Schellenberg's *Genres des mouches diptères. . . / Gattungen der Fliegen . . .* (1803), often emphasize their disturbingly segmented nature in life.

The distinctness-in-plurality of flies is often a feature of early illustrations, such as this one from Ulisse Aldrovandi, *De animalibus insectis libri septem . . .* (1638).

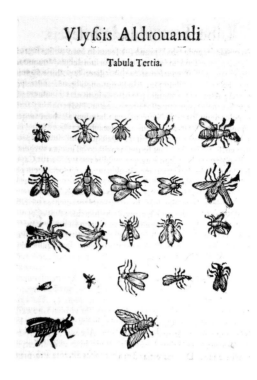

Vlyſsis Aldrouandi

Tabula Tertia.

But, unlike some of these creatures, the swarms of flies are simply the aggregations of individuals, rather than molar formations like ants' nests or beehives. There is no pack or swarm identity with flies.

So it is not surprising that flies prompt the sense of mathematical wonderment. The nineteenth-century entomologists William Kirby and William Spence estimated that an alarmed fly can travel about 30–35 feet (9–10.5 m) per second, which compares well with the 90 feet (27 m) per second of a racehorse. Scaling up the fly's speed in terms of its size produces prodigious values:

Our little fly, in her swiftest flight, will in the same space of time go more than the third of a mile. Now compare the infinite difference of the size of the two animals (ten millions of the fly would hardly counterpoise one racer), and how wonderful will the velocity of this minute creature appear! Did the fly equal the race-horse in size, and retain its present powers in the ratio of its magnitude, it would traverse the globe with the rapidity of lightning.[22]

Hooke rightly supposed that the note emitted by the fly indicated that its wings did not flap as quickly as those of the more high-pitched bee, but surmised that ''tis most probable that the quickest vibrating *spontaneous* motion is to be found in the wing of some creature'. A house fly beats its wings around 200–330 times a second. But this rapidity posed some mechanical questions.

[I]f we consider the exceeding quickness of these Animal spirits that must cause these motions, we cannot chuse but admire the exceeding vividness of the governing faculty or *Anima* of the Insect, which is able to dispose and regulate so the the motive faculties, as to cause every peculiar organ, not onely to move or act so quick, but to do it also so regularly.[23]

In fact, it has been difficult even for modern biologists, armed with a knowledge of internal neurochemical signalling, the modern equivalent of the animal spirits, to understand how flies and other insects employing even more rapid wingbeats can regulate a movement so fast – faster than any known nerve impulses can travel (human muscles can contract at most 10–11 times a second). The answer lies in the way in which the fly

Musca vibrans, the 'vibrating fly', was first described by Linnaeus in 1758. (The illustration here is from Donovan's *Natural History of British Insects*.)

harnesses a principle of recoil, As the wing moves downwards, its movement is resisted by the elasticity of the thorax to which it is attached. At the downpoint of the stroke, a 'click point' is reached, at which the resistance vanishes. The sudden relaxation of the muscles that have been contracting causes the wing to bounce upwards, the same process occurring in turn at the top of the wingbeat. Thus, it is not necessary for each wingbeat to be kept under synchronous nervous control: like a boxer's speed bag, the oscillatory motion need only be initiated and periodically renewed to sustain itself.[24]

Mathematics is never far away when flies are in the picture. Compared with the rates at which bacteria reproduce, fly-breeding may not seem very remarkable. And yet contemplating the reproductive capacities of flies regularly brings on slow paroxysms of amazed calculation. Campaigners for the fly's eradication saw a particular advantage in not underestimating these rates. F. W. Fitzsimons gives his reader the pleasure of following through his workings generation by generation. Assume a fly lays 150 eggs in a session, he says:

> Supposing these flies all hatch and eventually emerge as adult flies, which are allowed to breed unchecked; then the progeny of that single fly will amount to something like 6,488,560,000,000. Sometimes the original parent dies after laying one batch, but as likely as not she will lay two or three more batches of eggs. If she does, then these figures must be multiplied by three. Work it out and the total will stagger the imagination even of an astronomer.[25]

The same writer notes that, following a successful campaign of fly-eradication in Johannesburg in 1913, which 'accomplished the death of 61,943,000 flies', there must have been in the following summer season, 67,901,083,980,428,722,176,000,000, 000,000,000 fewer flies on the Rand than there might otherwise have been (pp. 72–3). Another way of evoking the appalling fertility of the fly is to imagine the depth of earth that could be covered in flies. The uninhibited progeny of a single couple of flies over a summer would be enough to cover the earth to a depth of more than 20 feet (6 m) in flies, goes one thrilling

This decanter used to catch flies suggests how quickly they can multiply, even in death.

estimate. According to another, the offspring of one pair of flies would fill the void between the Earth and the Sun.[26]

This oscillation of orders of magnitude is a constitutive part of the way in which the fly is imagined. The fly not only prompts reflection on the relationship of different scales, it seems to stand at a kind of hinge point between maximal and minimal. It became a commonplace in popular biological writing in the middle of the nineteenth century to identify the fly as a kind of cosmic median between the unimaginably large and the inconceivably small. The author of one such book, Leo H. Grindon, took the fly's measure relative to *Monas crepusculum*, in the mid-nineteenth century the smallest identified living organism, and the earth's largest animal:

A fly, somewhat improbably and inefficiently being attacked by a man with a spear, from the Gorleston Psalter of c. 1310–25.

The animal which holds the middle place in the scale of size, reckoning from the *Monas crepusculum*, the minutest to which our microscopes have yet reached, is the common house-fly. That is, there are as many degrees of size between the house-fly and the Monas, reckoning *downwards*, as, reckoning, upwards, there are between the house-fly and the whale.[27]

Great persons should not with their might,
Oppresse the poorer, though they might.

Who notes the noble bird that doth command,
All feathered fowles subiected to the skies,
And hath the Eagles princely nature scand,
Which doth disdaine to litigate with flies;
Hereby may weigh and wisely vnderstand,
In base contention little honour lies.
    For he that striueth with th'inferiour sort,
    Shall with dishonour reape an ill report.

Sometimes the fly suggested even larger perspectives:

It is commonly supposed that the telescope, in penetrating the unmeasured depths of space, and bringing into view systems of worlds, in which our sun with its planets is lost as a mere speck, gives us the most overwhelming conception of the grandeur of the universe, and of the infinite power and wisdom of God. But it may well be doubted whether the revelations of the microscope are not still more wonderful. The world beneath us is as great as the world above us. It is estimated that the common house fly occupies the central point in the scale of animated nature as far as our earth is concerned.[28]

Henry Baker's reflections on the relativity of the size of animals extended beyond space to the sense of time. Not only does every creature have equal room in proportion to its own size ('minute Animalcules in a Drop of Water, swim about with as much Freedom as Whales do in the Ocean'), but tiny creatures that live a short time may experience such a swift succession of ideas and mental impressions that they 'may be supposed, from the Number and swift Succession of Ideas suited to all these Purposes, to live as long, according to their own Thinking, as other Creatures do, where the same Train of Ideas proceeds more slowly, and takes up many Years'. [29]

Mark Twain, on the other hand, who found it unaccountable that nature should have taken so much trouble to evolve so troublesome and seemingly useless a creature as the fly, also found occasion to protest against the disproportionate role of the fly in creation. In his *Letters from the Earth* of 1909, Twain recounts the story of Noah's Ark, the survival of which is jeopardized by the fact that it is so slow in setting sail:

> He would have sailed at once, but the upholsterers and decorators of the house fly's drawing room still had some finishing touches to put on, and that lost him a day. Another day was lost in getting the flies aboard, there being sixty-eight billions of them and the Deity still afraid there might not be enough. Another day was lost in stowing forty tons of selected filth for the flies' sustenance.[30]

The rescue of Creation is further threatened by the fact that, on the third day, it is discovered that a fly has been left behind. The teeming Ark is compelled to pick its way back, and to search the inundated strands and mountain tops until the precious creature is found. Twain's sardonic disgust at the pleasure shown

Proboscis of a blow fly. Blow flies, or, as they are also known, 'bottle flies' (bluebottle, greenbottle, bronzebottle), commonly spread diseases through regurgitation of the excrement and other infected matter on which they feed.

in the rescue of the dipterous prodigal is the inverse of the fabled care shown by the Almighty for the fall of a single sparrow:

> after sixteen days of earnest and faithful seeking, the fly was found at last, and received on board with hymns of praise and gratitude, the Family standing meanwhile uncovered, out of reverence for its divine origin. It was weary and worn, and had suffered somewhat from the weather, but was otherwise in good estate. Men and their families had died of hunger on barren mountain tops, but it had not lacked for food, the multitudinous corpses furnishing it in rank and rotten richness. Thus was the sacred bird providentially preserved [p. 25].

The fly is both comically singular and horrifyingly legion, and seems to be the vehicle of Twain's charge that Creation is fundamentally out of joint, as a result of the blinkered obsessions of the Almighty. The charge is brought home by the revelation of the particular providence demonstrated in the fly's miraculous survival. For its role is not to make the roster of the 34 billion or so different species complete, but to ensure the survival of another, and even more incomprehensibly destructive organism, the bacterium that is the cause of 'a certain invaluable disease' – typhoid.

5 Fly Wars

Flies have never had straightforwardly positive associations, and have been associated with dirt and disease in many cultures. Long before the role of certain flies in transmitting disease was verified – the tsetse as the vector of sleeping sickness, the mosquito of malaria – flies were widely suspected of transmitting pathogens. A Talmudic reference indicates that the Jews saw flies as carriers of disease, though the disease concerned appears to be venereal.[1] The Hebrew word for hornet is suggestively close to the word used in the Old Testament for a skin condition usually translated as leprosy. Pliny reported in his *Natural History* that the Eleans seek from the gods a remedy against swarms of plague-bringing flies.[2] Thomas Sydenham thought he saw a correlation between numbers of flies and levels of disease:

> I have remarked that, if swarms of insects, especially houseflies, were abundant in the summer, the succeeding autumn was unhealthy. This I observed to be the case during the whole summer of the aforesaid year [1661]; whilst in the summers of the two following years, which were very healthy, the insects were very few.

However, he added a cautious rider to this: 'Still I must remark, that at the approach of even so serious a disease as the plague

A poster urging the use of fly-traps against tsetse flies.

itself, they were not observed to be very abundant.'[3] This is a remarkable observation, for it would take more than three centuries to confirm that bubonic plague is one of the very few diseases to which flies themselves are susceptible.

And yet flies have also been seen as having therapeutic uses. We saw in the last chapter that flies were associated both with eye disease and eye care. Muhammad ibn Musa Ad-Damiri, the author of the first attempt in Arabic literature to give a systematic account of natural history, reports: 'I have carefully examined the fly, and found that it defends itself with its left wing, which is the one supposed to contain a [cause of] disease,

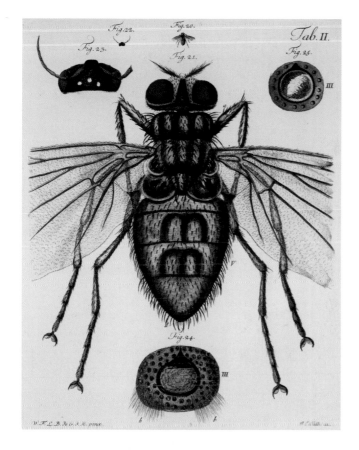

A house fly, from von Gleichen-Russworm, *Geschichte der gemeinen Stuben-fliege* (1790).

just as the right one is supposed to contain a remedy [for it].'[4] In the Middle East, flies were roasted and ground into a powder, which was rubbed on the skin against insect bites.[5] Pliny recommended the application of 'fresh heads of flies', or 'a paste made of fly ash, woman's milk and cabbage' to bald patches, and was followed in this advice by Galen and Aldrovandi and, as late as 1742, F. C. Lesser, who stated that flies are 'emollient, abstergent, and bring about hair growth: they are applied, crushed up, to the bald patch'. Rather less surprisingly, Lesser also testifies to the value of flies as a purgative.[6] Pliny also thought that a boil could be cured by rubbing into it an odd number of flies, and that flies mixed with hen's dung or bat's blood were sovereign against vitiligo.[7]

The growth of understanding during the nineteenth century of the bacteriological nature and transmission of many diseases made the fly humanity's great entomological antagonist. The first substantial links between flies and disease were established with blood-sucking or parasitic flies. In 1879 Patrick Manson observed the development of the worm *Filaria sanguinis hominis*, which causes elephantiasis, in the mosquito and pointed to the possibility that it might transmit the disease. Bloodsucking flies of the genus *Glossina* (tsetse fly) were linked conclusively to the spread of sleeping sickness by David Bruce in 1895. In 1900

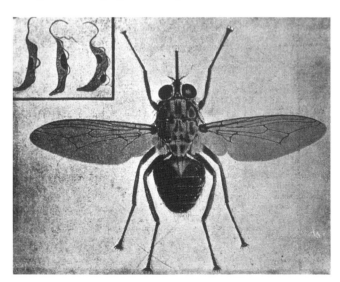

When David Bruce (1855–1931) demonstrated that the disease nagona, similar to human trypanoso-miasis or sleeping sickness, was caused by a parasite, or try-panosome, transmitted from antelopes to cattle by the tsetse fly, *Glossina morsitans*, it was the first demonstration that an insect carried a proto-zoan of a patho-logical kind.

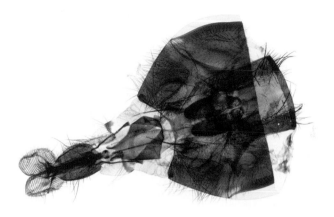

Blow fly head and tongue.

Walter Reed confirmed the suggestion of the Cuban scientist Carlos Finlay, first made in 1881, that yellow fever was transmitted by mosquitoes. The programme of eradication stimulated by his work made it possible to complete the building of the Panama Canal, which French engineers had abandoned in the 1880s, in part because of the problem of disease. From the 1890s onwards it began to be suspected that non-bloodsucking flies might also have a role in the transmission of disease. Houseflies do not have mouthparts that allow them to ingest solid matter, so have to dissolve their food into an acidic puddle at their feet. The habit of house flies of cleaning their eyes and mouthparts with their legs where bacteria could be trapped by the stiff bristles, along with the famed stickiness of the fly's foot, suggested to many that this would make it easy for them to act as the transmitters of many diseases. The principal diseases of which the fly was suspected of being the carrier were dysentery, typhoid, cholera and tuberculosis but, as the suspicions and evidence grew, other diseases, such as polio, were also added to the charge sheet.

LES MOUCHES

Les Mouches pondent dans le fumier, les matiéres fécales, les détritus de cuisine, les ordures, les gadoues et les substances animales ou végétales en voie de décomposition.

Les Mouches sèment plus **la mort...** que les gothas

La Mouche vous apporte :
la Fièvre typhoïde, la Diarrhée infantile, la Dysenterie, le Choléra, la **Tuberculose**, la Diphtérie, la Fièvre scarlatine, la Rougeole, l'Erésipèle.

Ce sont **les Mouches** qui apportent à vos **Bébés** les **Maladies** dont ils **meurent** !

OUTWITTED by COMMUNITY SANITATION

COMMUNITY SANITATION *planning keeps* FLIES *away from deadly disease germs with the* • • • • • MODERN APPROVED SANITARY PRIVY *Concrete Floor and Foundation*

A French anti-tuberculosis campaign poster, c. 1918.

A Federal Art Project poster promoting sanitary facilities in Illinois in the 1930s.

The role of the fly in the transmission of typhoid was particularly closely considered. The typhoid bacillus had been discovered in 1880, and first isolated and cultivated in 1884. It was a major cause of death among American troops in the Spanish-American war, in what has been called 'self-inflicted germ warfare', even though hostilities lasted for only four months, from July to November 1898.[8] It was observed that soldiers in screened tents fell ill less often and a US Government Report of two years later presented other convincing evidence of the role

As this late 19th-century advertising image showing a baby frolicking among flies suggests, flies acquired their fearsome reputation relatively recently.

of flies in the transmission of the disease. 'To those who have seen flies feeding upon fecal matter smeared over the buttocks of patients or have seen them crawling into the mouths of the unconscious typhoid subject, nothing more is necessary than to mention this possible means of the dissemination of the disease', it reported.[9] This led to a campaign, which met with success for a while, to change the name of *Musca domestica* from the cosy 'house fly' to the uncompromising 'typhoid fly'. The association between typhoid and the fly is sourly reprised in a poem by Samuel Beckett of 1934, which says of an apparently unemployed house fly that 'he could not serve typhoid and mammon'.[10] Sydenham's seventeenth-century observations were borne out by studies in 1910 that seemed to show a correlation between the prevalence of flies and the levels of dysentery.[11]

Between 1890 and 1920 the reputation of the fly changed entirely: from being an annoying but harmless, sometimes even cute nuisance, the fly became the subject of ruthless campaigns of extermination.[12] In 1862 the writer of an article on flies in *All the Year Round* could remark that 'It is a blessing . . . that pestilential filth should be . . . converted into comparatively harmless flies. By the wonderful transformability of matter, what would breed an infection grows into myriads of happy creatures.'[13] Twenty years later F. W. Fitzsimons, in his unambiguously titled *The House Fly: A Slayer of Men*, was asserting with confidence that 'we now know the House Fly to be the principal carrier of the germs of infectious diseases from the sick to the healthy'.[14] The very familiarity of the fly intensifies the danger it poses: 'the presence of five hundred cobras scattered throughout a city would be as nothing in comparison to the awful, the appalling danger and risks incurred by the presence of the common House Fly' (p. 4).

The killing of flies was now more than prudence or venial sadism: according to Fitzsimons, it was a civic and moral duty. He warns darkly that 'if every possible effort is not made to keep the house free of flies, *those responsible in that house are morally guilty should one or more members sicken and die in consequence of infection conveyed into the dwelling by flies*' (p. 25). Often recalling the slaying of the Egyptians by the plague of flies, texts like Fitzsimons's become biblical in their injunctions to holy war against the house fly: 'Our folk are falling daily, smitten down by microbes carried to them by the House Fly. Therefore, Arise and Smite – slay without mercy. Let your battle cry be, "Death to the Fly"'(p. 37).

The threat represented by the fly involved more than the spread of microbes through the human population. It also brought different parts of that population into intolerable proximity:

> It is a daily sight to see Kafirs, low-class Europeans, and others suffering from tuberculosis, bronchitis, influenza, syphilis, &c., expectorate yellow phlegm in the gutter and road, and to observe House Flies swarming around and on it. After walking through and wallowing in these masses of filth, teeming with microbes, the flies take wing and enter the nearest open window or door [p. 14].

Fitzsimons's counterpart in the UK was Edward Halford Ross, whose book *The Reduction of Domestic Flies* (1913) made no bones about the extent of the suffering caused by flies, which he straightforwardly blamed for the death of 1,800 infants in an epidemic of enteritis in London in 1910. Where the dominant

The Angel of Death is ever in your midst, sowing his seed of Death, and you know him not.
The Disease Microbe Army make such terrible attacks upon the human race, that few reach the allotted span of life. The soldiers of the Microbe Army cannot walk, fly or jump. The House Fly is their chief means of transport from man to man, whom they are ever seeking to kill.
Arise! and slay the Fly, and by so doing conquer this mighty Microbe Army. A human being is dying every second of time somewhere in the world, slain by microbes carried by House Flies. Arise, ye slaves! and glut your ire.

The fly as the Angel of Death, from Fitzsimons's *The House Fly: A Slayer of Men* (1915).

'The Fly is as Deadly as a Bomber!' – a wartime Philadelphia Department of Public Health poster warning against the danger of flies, 1941–3.

note of Fitzsimons's book is hysterically militant disgust, Ross evidences more complex feelings towards the fly, which include the sense of humiliation that humanity should be at the mercy of so tiny and contemptible a creature. '[I]t is a wonderful thing', wrote Ross, 'to consider that house-flies should have been the means of the prolongation of war, the expenditure of many lives and much money; and the cause – a tiny creature like the domestic fly. The idea would be almost ludicrous were it not so pitiful and humiliating.'[15] Where Fitzsimons issued a straightforward declaration of war against the fly, Ross sought to mobilize moral disapproval. The fly is represented as almost wilfully unhygienic: '[T]he fly likes to live in the midst of plenty, and the more filthy the food she has sticking to her mouth and legs the better she enjoys it. The germs like it too, for the fly never has a bath. It is a grand dirty life for all concerned'. But Ross also borrows some of Ruskin's admiration for the independent spirit of the fly, though representing it now as hedonistic irresponsibility: 'Each fly is king of his own country. He knows no laws or conventions, he can go where he likes and feed where he likes' (p. 34).

The incrimination of flies in the transmission of many diseases also encouraged some unfounded suspicions, most conspicuously in the case of poliomyelitis, which caused terrifying epidemics in the USA and Europe, culminating in the epidemic of 1916, which caused 27,000 cases and 6,000 deaths across the USA. Assuming that unsanitary conditions would provide ideal conditions for the incubation and transmission of the disease,

An advertisement for a flytrap in the form of a lighthouse, Boston, 1859. The ingenious device, whose shape suggested the eye of a fly, was made to rotate by means of clockwork, and even incorporated a reservoir of water in which to drown the flies.

Spraying the breeding sites of flies was a vital part of the campaign to control their numbers.

researchers investigating outbreaks in New York City were puzzled by the fact that cases seemed in fact to be spread randomly through the population, with children from clean, middle-class homes nearly as likely to contract the disease as children from the congested, insanitary homes of the poor and immigrants. As Naomi Rogers has shown, the fly provided these researchers with a way out of their perplexity, as well as a way of preserving the belief in the association between dirt and disease. For, in keeping with their reputation for bringing together what should be kept apart, flies could be identified as the means whereby the disease was transmitted to affluent homes that were otherwise thought to be sanitary and safe: 'it was not the fault of middle-class parents with a paralyzed child if a germ-carrying fly had traveled from the worst parts of the city'.[16] It would take some time to become clear that in a sense excessive hygiene rather than dirt was the problem. When polio is widespread, as it

112

probably was throughout the nineteenth century, infant exposure produces a mild form of the disease which confers life-long
immunity. As children became less likely to encounter the virus,
they had less immunity, and so were more likely to encounter
the disease at a later age, when complications such as paralysis
are more likely. Once again, the fly was the carrier, not just of
disease, but also of deeply held and long-cherished beliefs
about dirt, evil and irresponsibility.

The damage and danger represented by flies is far out-
weighed by the damage done by their larvae. The word 'vermin',
which comes from Latin *vermis*, a worm, is testimony to the

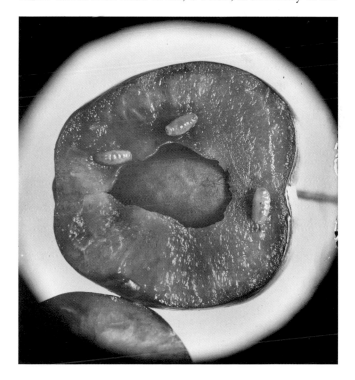

Fly larvae in
a cherry.

horror and suspicion with which maggots, grubs and worms have been viewed. Long before the discovery of bacteria, there were strong beliefs throughout the medieval period and beyond that worms were instrumental in causing disease in humans. Insect larvae have certainly been responsible for great economic destruction. One of the most damaging pests of the nineteenth century was the Hessian fly, described and classified by Thomas Say in 1817 as *Mayetiola destructor*, or the gall midge.[17] The fly, which is a small, black, mosquito-like insect in its adult state, first made its appearance on Staten Island around 1776, during the American War of Independence, and spread rapidly into Southern New York, Long Island and Connecticut, advancing at the rate of about 20 miles (32 km) a year. It is now found in all the major wheat-producing areas of the USA from the Atlantic coast to the Plains. It derives its name from the coincidence of its appearance shortly after the disembarkation on Staten Island of German mercenaries from the region of Hesse, under the command of Sir William Howe, who had been recruited by the British to assist in the efforts to subdue the American Revolution. Like many epidemics, plagues and infestations, the outbreak and spread of Hessian fly were attributed to and identified with the invaders, who, like many mercenary or irregular forces, were loathed because of their destructiveness. In fact, as Philip Pauly has recently shown, the name 'Hessian fly' was consciously chosen and propagated by one George Morgan, a colonel in the Revolution, and a wealthy New England farmer:

> The name of *Hessian* Fly was given to this insect by myself & a Friend early after its first appearance on Long Island, as expressive of our Sentiments of the two Animals – We agreed to use some Industry in spreading the name to add, if possible, to the detestation in which

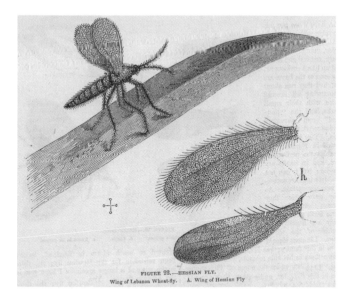

The so-called Hessian fly in a periodical illustration of 1859.

FIGURE 22.—HESSIAN FLY.
Wing of Lebanon Wheat-fly.   A. Wing of Hessian Fly

the human ~~Insect~~ [*sic*] was generally held by our yeomanry & to hand it down with all possible Infamy to the next Generation as a useful National Prejudice.[18]

Morgan's plan certainly worked, and the prejudice directed indifferently at the Hessian fly and the human its name recalled propagated as widely and efficiently as the fly itself. In 1862 Henry Ward Beecher was still to be found carefully distinguishing 'that hateful foreign fly' from the native house fly, 'every drop of whose blood is American', and lamenting that 'We could whip the British and the Hessians, but not the Hessian fly. *That* could never be brought to sign articles of peace.'[19]

In fact, as Philip Pauly has shown, the Hessian fly was at the centre of a series of shifts and struggles in which nature and nationality formed shifting patterns of alliance and antagonism.

The efforts to extirpate the Hessian fly formed part of the new Republic's efforts to rid itself of the treacherous and parasitic evils of the Old World. The arguments as to whether the fly had been brought over from Europe, or was a native of America that had for some reason only recently developed a taste for wheat, were an enactment of the argument between those who saw the new Republic as capable of purging itself from the corruption so endemic in Europe, and those who saw it as menaced from within by the cargo of original sin they carried within them.

Entomologists continued through the nineteenth century to investigate the Hessian fly and to speculate about its route into America. By the end of the century the consensus was that the fly had most likely evolved in Asia, travelled to Europe and been transported to America in the early 1770s, probably in the form of puparia, which are able to survive for up to a year. England managed to keep largely clear of Hessian fly until 1886, when it was discovered more or less simultaneously in Hertford and Inverness. Within a year it had spread across large areas of south-east England, the Midlands and Scotland. By this time, however, techniques developed in America for dealing with the fly limited the damage caused by the outbreak.[20] In Britain, wheat sowing was later than in the USA, so that most of the flies had died by the time the wheat sprouted; as a result it was largely barley that was attacked. As before, the invasion prompted biopolitical reflections. Grant Allen began his popular exposition of the life-history of the Hessian fly: 'Our worst enemies are not always the most apparent ones. It is easy enough to build forts for the protection of our towns and harbours against French or Germans, but it is very difficult to devise means of defence against such insidious foreign invaders.'[21]

The Hessian fly and its human hosts form a typically intimate enmity, resulting in intricate patterns of diptero-human coaction. As so often, the fly has been a crosser of boundaries, both forming and loosening claims regarding origin, identity, affinity and antagonism. But fly larvae can get even more close-up and personal with human beings. When the larvae of flies colonize living tissue, it is known as myiasis, a term first coined by R. W. Hope in 1840.[22] In 1921 W. S. Patton proposed a division of myiasis into three types that are often still referred to today. First of all, there is obligatory myiasis, which is limited to a small number of species, the larvae of which are found only in living tissues. Semispecific myiasis is characteristic of flies that, though normally breeding in dead animal bodies, will also occasionally lay their eggs in the diseased or necrotic tissues of living animals. Finally, there is accidental myiasis, which is seen, for example, in the occasional cases of house flies that accidentally infest wounds.[23]

One example of an obligatory myiasis is provided by the bot fly, perhaps from Gaelic *botus*, or belly-worm, or *boiteag*, maggot, different species of which will develop by feeding on the flesh of horses and other animals. After arranging for delivery to its host by stowing away as an egg on a bloodsucking mosquito, *Dermatobia hominis* digs a burrow in the flesh of birds and mammals, including, as its name suggests, humans. Like many such maggots, it employs grapnel-like hooks to embed itself in its host's flesh, meaning that any attempt to dislodge it only binds it more tightly in place, or, even worse, tears it apart, leaving some of the body inside to encourage infection. The good news about the maggot, probably the only good news, is that it secures its feeding position by secreting an antibiotic that protects it and its food supply from fungus and bacteria, so that as long as it remains alive its wounds do not tend to become infected. The most effective treatment for infestation by the bot fly maggot involves placing a piece of raw meat over the wound. Since it breathes air, the suffocating maggot will eventually leave its host and burrow through the meat in search of air. If one can bear to leave the larva to its own devices, it will also in time drop out spontaneously once it has matured and burrow into the earth, ready for its pupation. Adrian Forsyth has written a vivid account of a biologist friend of his who decided to tolerate the presence of a bot fly maggot in his scalp for the insights it would give him into the operations of symbiosis.[24]

Perhaps the most terrifying and dangerous creature of this kind is the screw-worm, the fly of which lays its eggs on open wounds in living animals. The millimetre-long maggots, which hatch after about twelve hours, attach themselves to the wound with sharp mouth-hooks, where they feed for about five days, destroying tissue and agonizingly enlarging the wound, before dropping to the ground to form the pupal stage. In the meantime, however, the liquids they produce to assist their feeding will often attract more flies of the same species that lay further batches of eggs. Serious secondary infections can result from these huge infestations, leading in many cases to death. Humans are not immune from the attentions of screw-worm, as is indicated by the name given to the New World version of the insect by Charles Coquerel, a French physician who in 1858 described its devastating effects on prisoners in the penal colony of Devil's Island: he called it *Cochliomyia hominivorax*, *homnivorax* meaning 'man-eater'. Infestation of noses, eyes, ears and mouth can be fatal if left untreated; 55 human cases were recorded in an outbreak of screw-worm in Texas in 1935.[25]

There are reports of maggot-like infestations of humans from early times, the most dramatic being the horrifying phthiriasis, or 'lousy disease', in which human beings die in terrible, stinking torment as a result of insects multiplying in tumours under the skin. The disease was thought to be caused by spontaneous generation of insects from infected blood, hence its reputation as a divine punishment for wickedness. The tyrant Sulla was said to have died of the lousy disease, as was Herod the Great. Lactantius goes into great detail about the death suffered by the Christian-persecuting Emperor Galerius, in whom a malignant ulcer forming 'in his secret parts' spread throughout his body:

> Now *Worms* began to breed within him. The *Smell* that came from him was so noysom, that it was felt not only all over the *Palace*, but in the very *City* likewise; and the Passages of his *Urine* and *Excrements* were now mixed, all the *Membranes* being corroded that separated them. He was eat up by *Vermine,* and the whole Mass of his Body turned into an universal Rottennesse . . . Some living *Animals*, and others that were boild, were applied to the Putrified parts, to try if the heat would draw out the *Vermine*: and this indeed opened as it were a vast *Hive* of them: yet a second Imposthumation discovered yet a much greater *Swarm*, so that his *Guts* seemed to dissolve all into *Worms*.[26]

Later writers began to doubt these stories, which seem to have been invented to satisfy a human desire to believe that the bodies of the wicked produce their own corruption in the form of endogenous infestation. Some of the alleged sufferers from lousy disease may have been victims of acute scabies or pediculosis. Given the tendency to conflate mites, lice and worms, some of the more dramatic cases may also have been cases of myiasis of open wounds.[27]

But, just as flies have been believed to have medicinal uses, infestation with maggots can also have more benign effects.

The 'blue fly', employed by Dominique-Jean Larry to clean wounds, is seen here in Hooke's *Micrographia* – probably the blow fly *Phaenicia sericata*.

Dominique-Jean Larrey, the medical officer of Napoleon's Egyptian campaign, noted how effective the maggots of what he called the 'blue fly' could be in clearing wounds of infected or dead tissue.[28] John Forney Zacharias, a Confederate physician during the American Civil War, also used maggots to help clean out gangrenous flesh from wounds, and William Baer noticed similar effects among the soldiers in his care during the First

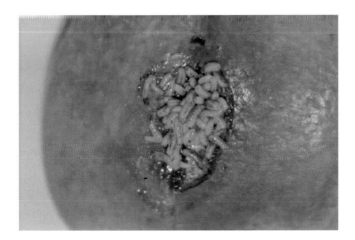

Larvae of the greenbottle, *Lucilia sericata*, at work clearing out diseased tissue from a cavity wound.

World War, and went on to use blow fly maggots to treat the lesions caused by osteomyelitis.[29] The difficulty was that there are only a few species of fly that will feed exclusively on diseased or necrotic tissue. The most common species employed were varieties of blow fly: *Lucilia sericata*, *Lucilia illustris* and *Phormia regina*. Infestation of wounds by other species of fly-larvae is extremely dangerous and, if maggots are to be used in any other than the desperate circumstances of the battlefield, it is important to ensure that they are bred under sterile conditions. There was great interest in the possibilities of maggot therapy during the 1930s, but it fell away with the development of antibiotics from the 1940s onwards. However, the increasing resistance of many organisms to antibiotics in recent years has rekindled an interest in the surrogate surgery that maggots can perform. As well as consuming diseased or dead flesh, maggots may secrete therapeutic agents such as urea and ammonium bicarbonate. Even patients who can adjust to the idea of these busy little helpers being set to work on them may nevertheless find the

A Russian poster warning against flies.

continuous wriggling extremely hard to bear. But this too may have a benefit, in that it can encourage exudation of fluids, which help to flush bacteria from the wound.[30]

Recently, Martin Monestier has described the fly as 'Man's worst enemy', although his highly dramatic account of the desperate battle between man and fly focuses more on the economic damage wrought by various invasions of flies.[31] Surprisingly, flies did not feature very much in the minor genre of entomophobic horror films that flourished in the nervous late 1950s.

Indeed, as we will see in the next chapter, the film by which the fly came to be best known, *The Fly* of 1958, followed by *The Return of the Fly* in 1959 and David Cronenberg's remake of 1986, makes the fly not a plague or a peril, but rather a kind of idiom or accent of the human. By then, as we are about to see, half a century of genetic investigation had made fly and human not so much antagonists as anagrams of each other.

6 Mutable Fly

Flies have often prompted reflections on the nature of form, mutability and making, partly because they have for so long been regarded as questionable creatures, as the form of the unformed, the figure of the faceless. There is something adventitious in the nature of the fly. Some myths of the creation of flies emphasize this sense of their accidental nature. A Chinese folk tale tells how the Lord of the Earth goes to visit the goddess Kuan Yin. Seeing everything in her dwelling spick and span, he grows jealous, rolls some paper into balls and says some magic words, at which they turn into flies, which buzz around and soil everything in the house (the goddess gets revenge by making ants to torment him in his sleep).[1] Even the Greek fly-god Myiagros, whose job it was to clear away flies during sacrifices to Zeus and Athena, can be regarded as what Hermann Usener called a 'momentary deity', a god conjured for a specific purpose and afterwards subsiding into inexistence.[2] Flies, like ticks, maggots and fleas, were believed for many centuries literally to be creations of chance, spontaneously generated from purulent matter. The belief in spontaneous generation was often linked to the belief that it produced imperfect creatures, which do not belong to the domain of divinely created nature. Aristotle assumed that, although such creatures could copulate and hatch offspring, these were 'never identical in shape with

This painted Chinese album leaf depicts the fly among the fauna and flora.

124

秋聲拂長林
寒蟬抱葉飛

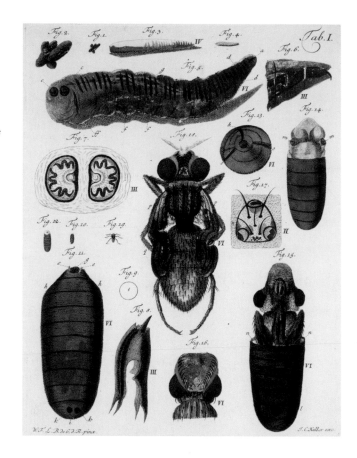

Stages in the life-cycle of the house fly, from von Gleichen's *Geschichte der gemeinen Stubenfliege*. Even though the life-cycle of flies seemed to be well understood, the belief that flies could be produced from spontaneous generation persisted for many centuries after Aristotle.

the parents, but a something imperfect'. From these hatchings, no animal can be produced but only 'nondescripts'. [3]

On one occasion, Aristotle imagines a kind of fly that is produced fully formed by spontaneous generation, reporting that 'In Cyprus, in places where copper-ore is smelted, with heaps of the ore piled on day after day, an animal is engendered in the fire, somewhat larger than a blue bottle fly, furnished with wings, which can hop or crawl through the fire.'[4] Pliny followed Aristotle, adding that the fly is called 'the *pyrallis*, or by some the *pyrolocon*. As long as it is in the fire it lives, but when it leaves it on a rather long flight it dies off.'[5] Now, the curious thing is that Aristotle knew the life-cycle of the fly perfectly well – copulation producing eggs, which turn into larvae, which pupate and metamorphose into flies. It seems that he thought that there were two kinds of flies, those generated spontaneously and incapable of reproducing themselves, and those reproducing by heredity. Lucian seems to share Aristotle's confusion when he writes that the fly is born 'as a maggot from the dead bodies of man or animals', which seems to suggest spontaneous generation.[6] But then he describes a straightforward process of growth and reproduction: 'Then, little by little, she puts out legs, grows her wings, changes from a creeping to a flying thing, is impregnated and becomes mother to a little maggot which is tomorrow's fly.'[7]

For many centuries, these two beliefs continued to coexist. Like other such insects, the fly, especially in its maggot stage, where it seems to have no determinate shape, exists between form and formlessness. Early religious attitudes towards the fly reflected this ambivalence about its constitution. Christianity saw the fly as emblematic of the imperfect world of mutable natural forms. St John Chrysostom was employing a common

Flies with their corresponding larvae and pupae, from Johannes Goedaert, *De insectis* (1685).

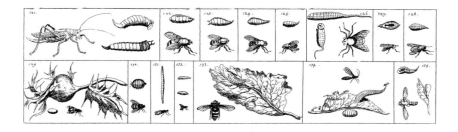

metaphor when he wrote that the soul absorbed in the thought of riches and other earthly preoccupations was 'a soul full of stupidity, which does not differ from flies or gnats, a soul crawling on the earth, wallowing in mire, unable to contemplate anything great'.[8] The fly's love of the light made it useful to contrast earthly with spiritual vision among Christian writers. In his response to the Manichean arguments of Faustus, Augustine writes: 'you swear by the light, which you love as flies do; but you think nothing of the light of the mind, so different from that of your eyes, which illuminates every person who comes into the world'.[9] It became a traditional consolation for those losing their sight to be told that they should hold in contempt a bodily faculty that they had in common with mere flies. Didymus the Blind of Alexandria, a learned man of the fourth century, confessed to St Anthony that the loss of his sight at the age of four had been a grief to him. The saint replied that 'he wondered how a wise man could regret the loss of that which he had in common with ants and flies and gnats, and not rather rejoice that he possessed a spiritual sight like that of the saints and Apostles'.[10]

The problem of the fly recurred regularly in debates between early Christians and those who defended the philosophy of the Greeks and Romans. One of the commonest ways of pouring scorn on the pagan philosophies of Plato, Pythagoras and others was to ridicule their views about the soul. St John Chrysostom wrote of Greek doctrines of the soul that they were full of disgrace, maintaining as they did that 'the souls of men will become flies, gnats or bushes, and that God himself is just such a soul, along with similar horrors'.[11] This is a favourite theme of Chrysostom's, who wrote in another homily that Plato 'threw away his life on useless and empty doctrines. What profit is there to know that the soul of the philosopher becomes a fly? A fly, right enough: but it's not that he has been changed into a fly, but rather that a fly has taken up residence in the philosopher's soul.'[12]

From the third century onwards, the rise and rapid spread of Manicheanism from the East presented Christians with a powerful rival cosmogonic system which required energy and ingenuity to rebut. The fly featured again in these arguments. Manicheanism presents Christians with a challenge that is the reverse of that offered by other pagan writers such as Celsus. Where Celsus had proposed a syncretism that saw God everywhere, the Manicheans restricted the reach of the divine, seeing the cosmos as cloven between the principles of light and darkness. Manicheans accused Christians of being evasive on the question of whether God had full dominion over the dark things of creation and substituting mystery for rational explication. This gave difficulty to the Christian apologist Arnobius, who lived in Sicca in North Africa and about 305 wrote a long defence of Christian theology against alternative beliefs entitled *Adversus gentes* (sometimes also known as *Adversus nationes*). He finds himself embarrassed by the difficult question of who, if not God, is to be credited with the creation of lowly forms like flies. Rather than admit the possibility either that God might have created such things, or that there might be some other, non-divine creative principle at work in them, he takes refuge in flummoxed sulks:

> are we bound to show whose they are, because we deny that they are God's? That by no means follows necessarily; for if we were to deny that flies, beetles, and bugs, dormice, weevils, and moths, are made by the Almighty King, we should not be required in consequence to say who made and formed them; for without incurring any censure, we may not know who, indeed, gave them being, and yet assert that not by the Supreme Deity were creatures

produced so useless, so needless, so purposeless, nay more, at times even hurtful, and causing unavoidable injuries.[13]

These attitudes survive, and the fly has continued to mark the point at which providence gives way to gratuity in creation. Ogden Nash's poem 'The Fly' remarks: 'God in His wisdom made the fly/And then forgot to tell us why.'[14] Mark Twain, whose contempt for the fly and its maker we have already encountered, declared that '[n]ot one of us could have planned the fly, not one of us could have constructed him; and no one would have considered it wise to try, except under an assumed name'.[15] However, a religious defence against the idea of a bifurcated Creation or blundering Creator begins to emerge in the work of Augustine, the first and probably the greatest Christian defender of the fly. Augustine, who had himself been a Manichean in his earlier years, explains the particular doctrinal risk posed by the case of the fly: 'Let no one fool you', he advises, 'when you are being tormented by flies. For some have been mocked by the devil, and taken in by flies. Just as hunters put flies in their traps to capture hungry birds, so these have been deceived with flies by the devil.' Once admit the Manichean argument that flies might not be part of God's creation and that there could be some other creative principle in the universe than God, it will prove very hard to draw the line of division between evil and divine creatures. Eventually, the rot of doubt will run all the way up the scale until one may be brought to deny the divine origin even of man himself:

A certain person was being pestered by flies; a Manichean came upon him in his suffering; and when he said that he could not bear the flies and loathed them intensely, the Manichean immediately said: 'Who made them?' And

Mutable flies
assail St Antony
in Lucas Cranach's
engraving of 1506.

since he was suffering from the vexation of the flies and
hated them, he did not dare affirm that God made them,
even though he was a Catholic. The Manichean continued
straight away, asking 'If God did not make them, who
did?' 'Truly,' said the other, 'I believe that the devil made
flies.' To which the other immediately replied, 'If the devil
made the fly, as I see you concede, because you have clear

understanding, who then made the bee, which is only a little larger than the fly?' He did not dare say that God made the bee, when he did not make the fly, since the two cases were so closely comparable. So from the bee, the Manichean drew him on to the locust, from the locust to the lizard, from the lizard to the bird; from the bird he led him on to the sheep, and thence to the cow, the elephant, and, finally, to man, and persuaded him, a man, that man was not made by God. Thus, assailed by flies, this wretched man was made into a fly, and the possession of the devil.[16]

In his own arguments against the Manicheans, Augustine repeatedly construes, indeed celebrates, the fly, not as the principle of troubling division within creation, but rather the proof that divine care extends all the way through it. Conceived as a creation of God, the lowliest creature is greater than the divisive principle of 'light' valued by the Manicheans:

And here, if, in their perplexity, they had asked me whether I reckoned that the soul even of a fly excelled that light, I would have responded 'Indeed it does.' Nor would it have intimidated me that the fly is so small, for I would just have been convinced that it is alive. For, if one wonders what causes such diminutive members to grow, what pulls so tiny a body here and there according to its natural appetites, what moves its feet in order when it runs, what governs and vibrates its wings in flight – then, whatever that might be, when properly considered, there is such towering magnitude in this tininess (*in tam parvo tam magnum eminet*), that it outdoes any lightning that could strike upon the eye.[17]

In representing the fly, not as a troubling aberration in creation, but as a miracle of rare device, Augustine inaugurates a new tradition in Christian thought about the natural world. Islamic writers also stressed the Inimitability of the divine workmanship In forming the fly: Ad-Dimiri's late fourteenth-century zoological lexicon repeats the claim that 'Verily, those on whom ye call beside God could never create a fly if they all united together to do it.'[18]

One of the earliest works of entomology in English, Thomas Moffet's *Theater of Insects* (1658), begins its discussion of flies by naming them '[t]hese little creatures so hateful to all men', but also finds much to admire in them: 'how strongly do those infirm creatures demonstrate the great power of God? For consider but the least Fly that is, and observe how in so little a body the most high God hath curiously fitted feet, wings, eyes, snout, and other parts, which yet are less than the least threed.'[19]

One of the most important developments for the understanding and appreciation of flies was provided by a famous experiment in 1688 by Francesco Redi, which cast doubt on the long-held view that maggots were bred spontaneously from decaying meat. Redi kept decaying meat in two containers, one sealed, the other open to the air. Only the one open to the air developed maggots, a clear indication that the maggots had come from elsewhere, namely the eggs laid upon the meat by flies.[20] As we have seen, the development of the microscope and its application for observation of the natural world verified Redi's suggestions and changed conceptions of insects and other diminutive creatures.

Among the most influential of the first observers of insects was the Dutch anatomist Jan Swammerdam, whose *Historia generalis insectorum* (1669) and *Biblia naturae: sive historia insectorum*, which did not appear until 1737, after his death, showed the fruits

In his *Esperienze intorno alla generazione degl'insetti* (*Experiments Relating to the Generation of Insects*) of 1688, Francesco Redi reported on his momentous experiments, showing that flies were not spontaneously generated from decaying meat, but hatched from eggs deposited by flies.

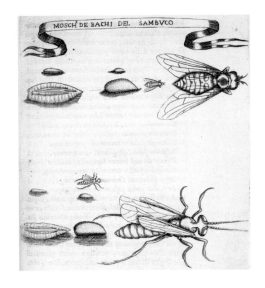

MOSCH DE BACHI DEL SAMBVCO

of long and meticulous observation and formed the basis for the classifications of insects, based upon reproduction and development, that we employ today. Much of Swammerdam's work had to wait until the 1750s to be translated into English, but a remarkable anticipation of that work did appear in 1681, in the form of a book entitled *Ephemeri Vita; or, the Natural History and Anatomy of the Ephemeron, a Fly That Lives But Five Hours*. The fly in question is now commonly known as the mayfly, though it is not a true, which is to say dipterous, fly. In fact, despite the subtitle of the work, Swammerdam showed that, though the flying form of the ephemeron may have a brief, if sportive life, the life-cycle of the creature lasts very much longer. Eggs deposited by the female into the water over which it flies hatch into larvae that dig themselves into the mud at the bed of the river, where they develop for three years before emerging as the adult fly. The extraordinary detail with which Swammerdam was able to describe the

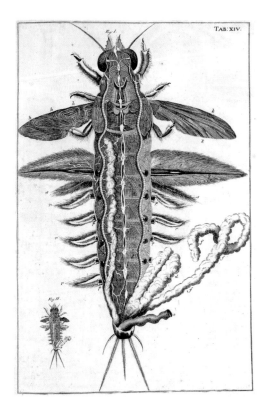

TAB:XIV.

The Ephemeron (mayfly), from John Swammerdam's *The Book of Nature, or The History of Insects* of 1758.

stages of the ephemeron's life and the intricacy of its construction led him to a round rejection of the prevailing view that such creatures were formed by chance;

> notwithstanding the Common Opinion that many Insects named Exangious, are chance-births, taking their original from Corruption, that is, out of the motion of the moisture and warmth which proceedeth from Corrupting matter, either in Inanimate or Sensitive Bodies, or Vegetables;

constant experience teacheth us the contrary, as, among other, appeareth in this account of the Production of the *Ephemeron*, which proceedeth from a Visible and known Seed, contrary to that false opinion of men prejudiced to the contrary, who believe they are Produced out of putrifying Clay and Water; as if such a *chance-Productor* had the power to produce a Creature in all Ages to be admired, and hardly by the most Ingenious and Wise to be described.[21]

Redi's experiments, confirmed by the observations of the early microscopists, simultaneously encouraged what we would recognize as a more scientific account of reproduction and shored up religious arguments about the necessity of a regulating divine intelligence. In the second of the Boyle lectures, endowed in his will by Robert Boyle to encourage discussion of the existence of

Metamorphoses of the fly, from Francesco Redi's *Experimenta circa generationem insectorum . . .* (1671).

God, Richard Bentley condemned the doctrine of spontaneous or 'aequivocal' generation as a central part of the mechanical philosophy of atheism: 'there is no one thing in the World, which hath given so much Countenance and Shadow of Possibility to the Notion of Atheism, as this unfortunate mistake about the aequivocal generation of Insects'.[22] He drew support from Redi's experiments of only four years previously, recalling that Redi had been unable to produce spontaneous generations from putrefying carcasses, even of insects themselves, when they were sealed in glass vessels: 'Even Flies crush'd and corrupted, when inclosed in such Vessels, did never procreate a new Fly: though there, if in any case, one would have expected that success.'[23] Bentley took particular pleasure in pointing out that, when flies were allowed access to the decaying matter, only fly-larvae of the permitted species appeared, even when the putrefying material was 'a mucilage of bruised Spiders', and took pleasure in asking: 'was not that a surprizing Transformation indeed, if according to the vulgar opinion, those dead and corrupted Spiders spontaneously changed into Flies?'[24]

The fly, and in particular the fly's foot, which was puzzled over by many observers and natural historians from Hooke onwards, became the symbol of the miraculous construction of disregarded and diminutive creatures, particularly among those advancing variants of the 'argument from design' for the existence of an omnipotent Creator. '[T]he Deity is as conspicuous in the structure of a Fly's paw, as he is in the bright Globe of the Sun himself', wrote the Abbé Pluche in his *Spectacle of Nature*, a popular and influential work showing the evidence of divine design in the natural world, which was first published in 1733 and reprinted throughout the eighteenth century.[25] Others, such as F. C. Lesser, found similar proof of the majesty of God in the perfection of his tiniest creatures such as the fly.[26]

The foot of
a house fly,
from Hooke's
Micrographia.

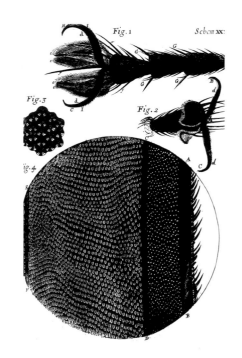

Artists like Georg-
Dionysus Ehret
(1708–1770),
endeavoured
to depict the
suddenly realized
beauty of the fly.

The fly's reputation continued to rise among Romantic writers, along with that of other insects and previously despised forms. Wordsworth describes the homely industry in the cottage of the shepherd Michael as 'Making the cottage through the silent hours/Murmur as with the sound of summer flies'. Pausing to contemplate a summer noon, The Wanderer in Wordsworth's *Excursion* reflects: 'while this multitude of flies/With tuneful hum is filling all the air;/Why should a tear be on an old Man's cheek?'[27] Later in the same poem, Wordsworth avoids the traditional disparagement of flies in contrast with industrious social insects like ants and bees, praising rather the spirit of 'participation by delight' that causes 'The gilded summer flies to mix and weave/Their sports together in the solar beam,/Or in the gloom of twilight hum their joy'.[28] (As we have seen, the older Wordsworth was capable of being much more censorious about flies' capacity for fornication.) Goethe, who devoted some considerable time to the scientific observation of *Musca domestica*, had his Werther experience the immanence of the divine in the little lives of insects: 'I sense the teeming of the little world among the stalks, the countless indescribable forms of the grubs and flies, closer to my heart, and feel the presence of the Almighty who created us in His image, the breath of the All-loving who bears us aloft in perpetual joy and holds us there.'[29]

Writing in 1896, Edward Poulson put into the mouth of a fly a rebuff to the arrogance of a biologist like François Raspail, who, anticipating modern ambitions, claimed that he could reproduce all Creation from a single living cell:

Pardon me, Monsieur Raspail, you and your ancestors have been looking at and admiring my little Foot for 230 years, and you are not able to come to any general agreement regarding the means by which I can walk on your glass window panes, how then can you justify your statement about reproducing 'all creation' from a living cellule! while you are unable to trace to their ultimate details the locomotive mechanism of my foot, and are still less able to describe its hidden wonders or to 'reproduce' it! [punctuation *sic*][30]

The appreciation of the fly's intricate form as a miracle of rare device had prompted attempts to produce mimic or artificial flies from medieval times. The French humanist Pierre Ramus writes that in Nuremberg the mathematician and astronomer Johannes Müller (*c.* 1436--1476), known as Regiomontanus, 'caused an iron fly to fly out from his hand, make a circuit of his dinner-guests and finally, as though wearied, to return to the hand of its master'.[31] The French poet Guillaume du Bartas expanded on this story in his epic retelling of the creation of the world, *La Sepmaine* (1578):

> Once, as this Artist (more with mirth then meat)
> Feasted some friends that he esteemed great,
> From under's hand an iron Fly flew out;
> Which having flowen a perfect Round-about,
> With weary wings, return'd unto her Master,
> And (as iudicious) on his arme she plac't-her.
> O divine wit! that in the narrow womb
> Of a small Fly, could finde sufficient room
> For all those Springs, wheels, counterpoiz, and chains,
> Which stood in stead of life, and spur, and rains.[32]

The fame of the poet Virgil was so great in the medieval world that many stories of his magical skills circulated. It is said that Virgil asked the Emperor Augustus whether a bird that could kill

This bronze fly, functioning as a table decoration in a restaurant in São Paulo, may allude distantly to the apotropaic function of Virgil's famed brass fly.

birds or a fly that could kill flies would be more desirable. Since Naples was at that time suffering from a plague of flies, the emperor stated a preference for the latter. Virgil constructed a brass fly on astrological principles, and prayed over it to the Roman god of flies, Myagros. He set it up on the gate of the city and, for the eight years that it remained, Naples was free of flies.[33] In some other stories, the tale is Christianized, with the feat being credited to a certain Bishop Virgilius, whose artificial fly kept the food from spoiling in the shops of Naples for eight years.[34]

Along with other insects, flies have featured strongly in the brooches, clasps, necklaces and other forms of jewellery of many civilizations. The British Museum has a superb Egyptian example, a necklace dating from the Eighteenth Dynasty (1470–1350 BC), made of flies interspersed with garnets. Though fly necklaces were given as a recognition of courage on the battlefield, their presence in tombs among the effects of notable women, such as the wives of Thuthmosis III, may have reflected a more generalized kind of honour accorded to the fly.

A watercolour of unidentified – and rather fanciful – flies, from an anonymous album (*c.* 1700) of watercolour drawings of insects.

Perhaps the affinity between flies and jewels stems in part from the fact that insects like the fly exhibit jewel-like characteristics even when alive; they seem hard, glittering, mineral, with nothing fleshly about them. Insects became particularly popular as jewellery motifs in Europe from the 1860s onwards. As one commentator noted in 1904:

The singular appearance of insects results not only from the tools and accessories with which they bristle, but also from the immobility of their countenances, from the absence of all expression in their faces. They are knights who have arrayed themselves in their most splendid vestments. Nothing is too beautiful for them: velvet and silk, precious stones and rare metals, superb enamels, laces, brocades, are lavishly used in their garments. Emeralds, rubies and pearls, golds dull and burnished, polished silver, mother-of-pearl mingle, chord or contrast with one another. They create the sweetest harmonies and the most daring dissonances.[35]

The jewelled associations of flies may be assisted by the fact that flies are among the many insects found petrified in amber. The fascination of such amber fossils derives perhaps from the contrast between the quick, darting flight of the fly and the strange, stately permanence of its glassy entombment. Robert Herrick's 'The Amber Bead' articulates something of this exquisite richness, in which the moment has become a monument:

I saw a Flie within a Beade
Of Amber cleanly buried:
The Urne was little, but the room
More rich then *Cleopatra's* Tombe.[36]

The affinity between flies and artifice is suggested by the trope of the 'gilded fly', a phrase which, as we saw in chapter Three, first appears in *King Lear* (IV. 6). The 'gilded fly' is sometimes taken to mean a butterfly, although the original context, in which Lear thinks of a fly openly copulating in his royal sight,

Two flies in amber.

A woodland hover fly (*Ferdinandea cuprea*) displays its glistening metallic wings and body.

suggests the metallic glister of a bluebottle or blow fly. The gilding of flies is sometimes taken as a sign of how finely worked nature is, even in its meanest forms. 'Nature's self, in all her pictures fair,/Colours her Insect works with nicest care,/Nor better forms, to please the curious eye,/The spotted Leopard than the gilded Fly', we read in William Hayley's 'Essay on Painting'.[37] But the gilded fly also became associated with vain ostentation or meretricious, deceitful display, designed to curry favour or inveigle unsuspecting prey. 'These with a gilded fly we snare, /With gilded flatt'ry those are won', muses the fair adventurous Chloe in a moralistic little satire by Charles Hanbury Williams, but continues with the warning: 'ah, fair fools! beneath this shew/Of gaudy colours lurks a hook!'[38]

It is in the art of angling that most elaborate forms of artificial fly have been developed. The first mention of fishing with an artificial fly is found in Aelian's *De natura animalium*, where he says it is practised in a river in Macedonia.[39] The next is not for over a thousand years later, when the *Treatyse of Fysshynge with an Angle* was published by Dame Juliana Berners, prioress of Sopwell near St Albans. Her short book contains patterns for twelve flies to be used between March and August, including the Stone Fly, the Dun Fly and the Wasp Fly. In his notes to John Dennys's poem *The Secrets of Angling* (1613), William Lawson explains that fishing for trout requires an artificial fly, which

The first published drawing of an artificial fly, from John Dennys's *The Secrets of Angling . . .* (1613).

> must counterfait the Mayflie which is bred of the Cod-bait, and is called the Waterflie, you must change his colour every month, beginning with a darke white and so grow to a yellow. The forme cannot so well be put on paper as it may be taught by sight: yet it will be like this forme – [40]

At this point he inserts the first published illustration of an artificial fly. Thereafter the art of fly-tying can be traced through

The striking colours of *Alophora hemiptera*, a tachinid fly, the larvae of which are parasitic on crickets and grasshoppers.

works like Thomas Barker's *Barker's Delight; or, The Art of Angling* in 1659 and Richard Franck's *Northern Memoirs*, which provides one of the earliest accounts of fishing for salmon using a fly.[41] Isaac Walton was not a very experienced fly fisher, and contented himself with reproducing Juliana Berners's twelve fly-patterns. But these were considerably augmented by patterns for 65 flies for catching trout and grayling provided by Charles Cotton in the supplementation of Walton's *The Compleat Angler* that he published in 1676.[42]

As it has evolved since the sixteenth century, the tying of artificial flies – principally for the fishing of trout and grayling and then, increasingly from the nineteenth century onwards, of salmon – has become more complex, controversial and differentiated. All are agreed on the central principle that an artificial fly should resemble a natural fly sufficiently well to deceive a fish into taking it. But it is by no means clear quite what resemblance means. For one thing, there is the choice of fly from among the species that abound in or near rivers. Then the changes undergone by flies during their complex life-cycles enjoin careful consideration of which stage of the fly's development to choose, along with how to synchronize with prevailing weather conditions. Up until the middle of the nineteenth century, most fly fishing was of the 'wet-fly' variety, involving a lure that floated just below the surface of the water. Although fish will undoubtedly take flies that have fallen into the water in this manner, and will also feed on insects whose early stage of development takes place in water, many prefer live flies snapped in flight from just above the water. Thus, as one connoisseur haughtily maintains, 'wet-fly fishing, strictly speaking, is mostly not *fly* fishing at all but nymph or larva fishing'.[43] Besides which a 'wet-fly' will quickly lose its carefully designed verisimilitude once it has become waterlogged. The first half of the nineteenth century saw the development of dry-fly fishing, in which the lure is made to float on or hover just above the surface of the water. If this kind of artificial fly had the advantage of keeping its shape and colour, many more considerations came into play in its construction. For the lure had now not only to resemble the form of a fly, but also to suggest its characteristic movements and its changing appearance under different conditions of light, wind and weather.

On top of this, there were more epistemological considerations. Two schools of thought gradually formed regarding the mimesis of the artificial fly, the realist and the impressionist. The realist school considered that the most effective fly was one that resembled its original, as it seems to human eyes. The impressionist school, which began to develop during the early years of the twentieth century, tried to construe instead what the trout or other target fish might be seeing. As May Berenbaum drily observes, '[o]btaining the perspective of a fish is a complex mental exercise'.[44] The impressionist school of fly-tying arose in parallel with experiments in perception and perspective taking place in other areas of cultural life, such as psychology, painting and warfare. One of the earliest arguments in favour of impressionism in fly-tying, J. C. Mottram's *Fly Fishing: Some New Arts and Mysteries*, appeared in 1915, the year that the word 'camouflage' entered the English language.[45]

All these considerations have brought about in the world of fly fishing a growing autonomy from the actuality of flies' biological existence or appearance. The universe of artificial flies constitutes a kind of 'second nature' or parallel universe, in which, for example, the different stages of the mayfly's development are represented by distinct kinds of artifical fly: nymph, dun, spinner and spentwing. For all the efforts to exploit the entomological knowledge that accrued during the nineteenth

The Bangkok Blue
fishing fly.

The Mardi Gras
fishing fly.

The Bhutan Fan
fishing fly.

century, artificial flies have grown more and more into a separate order of simulacra, with its own history and subject to its own rules of evolution, selection, adaptation, multiplication and decline. Perhaps the most telling sign of this is the division that has sometimes been made by anglers between 'special flies', which imitate an individual species; 'general flies', which imitate the shared characteristics of several species; and the controversial 'fancy flies', which imitate 'not a species nor a genus nor a group, but fly life generally'.[46] Although many purists have looked down on the fancy fly – 'the use of such flies debases dry-fly fishing as it has wet-fly fishing, which has only recently begun to throw off this falsehood, and already is becoming a better and purer sport', one commentator has growled[47] – there is a sense in which all such artificial flies really belong to this 'unnatural history'. Looking at images of classic salmon flies, with names like The Lady Caroline, The Purple King, The Evening Star, The Pitcroy Fancy, The Bhutan Fan, Mardi Gras, The Mystery and The Spirit Fly, one is led away from entomology to the poetic evocation of artifice found in W. B. Yeats's poem 'Sailing to Byzantium' (Yeats himself being the author of an admiring poem about an imaginary fly fisherman): 'Once out of nature I shall never take/My bodily form from any natural thing'.[48]

More recently, researchers have begun attempting to simulate, not just the form and appearance of the fly, but also its action and behaviour, with the complexities of fly flight being a particular preoccupation. The fly is a favoured comparator when it comes to naming model aeroplanes and other flying devices – for example the 'Stubenfliege', a model plane advertised by a German company in 2001. Researchers have taken to constructing various kinds of artificial fly, or fly simulator, in order to investigate the flight patterns and capabilities of flies, and to

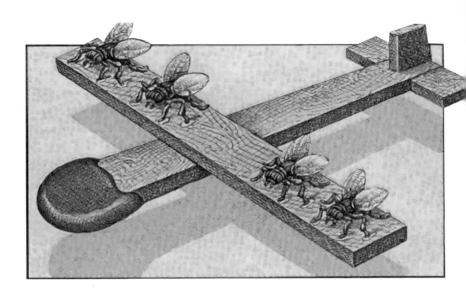

Flies learning the value of cooperative effort.

harness their capacities.[49] Michael Dickinson of the University of California at Berkeley has built various models to enable him to simulate and analyse the flight of flies, including a model of the wings of a *Drosophila* fly called Robo-fly and a prototype micromechanical flying insect (MFI).[50] Some versions of this endeavour are unashamed variants of the schoolboy's cruelty, such as the spoof instructions given on one website for constructing a house fly-powered aeroplane: house flies are refrigerated into a comatose state, glued to the wing of a plane formed from two matchsticks, and revived in order to learn the virtue of cooperation. Others are much less homespun. Philip Pullman's *Northern Lights* features a furiously buzzing clockwork spy-fly which pursues the fleeing children.[51]

But the most dramatic change in the status of the fly has come about in the area of genetic research. The end of the nineteenth century saw a move from a biology based upon inferences drawn from precise observation of animals in their habitats to a biology based upon experiment and demonstration. The dominance of experimental as opposed to observational biology meant that by the beginning of the nineteenth century flies were often employed, alongside other organisms such as mice, birds and worms, in laboratory-based experiments. In 1907 the biologist Thomas Hunt Morgan, newly arrived at Columbia University, saw the potential of flies for investigations into the biology of inheritance. His first use of the fly was to test the theory of the inheritance of acquired characteristics, first proposed in the earlier part of the nineteenth century by J. B. Lamarck, who believed that organisms evolved new bodily forms and functions in response to changing needs and conditions, and could pass these new forms on to their descendants. Morgan's student, Fernandus Payne, bred 49 generations of fruit flies that had never been permitted to see the light of day. When he looked to see whether this had resulted in any reduction in the size of their eyes or visual function, he found none.

The most important reason that the evolutionary biology of the nineteenth century had been descriptive and theoretical rather than experimental was that evolution required such long periods of time. The great advantage of the fly, and one fly in

A fruit fly of the genus *Drosophila*.

particular, the diminutive fruit fly, *Drosophila* ('dew-lover') *melanogaster*, was that it compressed the long, aching aeons required for evolutionary change into a matter of months or weeks. Once again, the fly was bringing together what had previously been incommensurable scales. *Drosophila* proved to be cheap and easy to breed in the laboratory; in many places in the world, one has only to leave out a milk bottle with a humming piece of rotting banana in it to whistle up an eager contingent of laboratory subjects. *Drosophila* was continuously fertile and prolific, producing a new generation every 30 days; male and female were easily distinguishable; and it had only four chromosomes.[52]

To begin with, Thomas Hunt Morgan had little interest in evolutionary theory, and was unimpressed by the theories of biological inheritance that other biologists were actively developing out of Gregor Mendel's experiments with pea plants. However, in 1910 the sudden appearance among Morgan's samples of fruit flies with white rather than the usual red eyes kindled in him a curiosity to see how the mutation might be passed on. When he bred several generations of the mutant flies, he found that the distribution of inherited characteristics strongly confirmed the heredity models devised by Mendel.[53]

Soon, Morgan was breeding flies on an industrial scale, in order to maximize the number of new and interesting mutants he had to work with. Studying their patterns of inheritance allowed him and his associates to start developing genetic maps showing how genes for particular characteristics were arranged in specific positions on the fly's chromosomes. All of this was dependent upon the principle that the more flies you had available, the greater the likelihood of mutant flies; and mutations allowed the investigator to understand normal genetic functioning through instances where it went wrong. Thus the very

PLATE 37.

J.O.Westwood delt.

Lizars sc.

1. Asilus abdominalis.
2. Acanthomera immanis.

Cartoon by
Andrew Toos.

"I appreciate what you've done for science ...
now drop the bonus request, or I'll swat you."

principle of mutativeness that made Aristotle and his followers see flies as deficient in essential form became a central part of what fruit flies offered to the genetic researcher. In fact, for all the thousands of flies he bred, Morgan found it difficult to generate enough mutations, since he did not have a reliable method for producing them, though variations in temperature at crucial moments in the flies' development yielded some results. In a sense, he was still reliant upon a principle of spontaneous generation, or nonce-production. This was to change in 1926, when Hermann Muller, who had worked with Morgan at Columbia, began experimenting with the effects of x-rays, and discovered that bombarding flies with radiation produced hugely increased numbers and kinds of mutation. Where Morgan had managed to pick out around 400 usable mutations from the 20 million or so flies he had bred since 1910, Muller was able to produce nearly that number in a single day. This made it possible to study the effects of mutations in entire populations, opening up a new perspective in genetic studies.

Muller, who was to win the Nobel Prize for his work in 1946, became concerned about the dangers of x-ray radiation, and campaigned vigorously for greater protections for those exposed to it and to other forms of radiation. Muller's anxieties

A sequence of flies suggesting their mutability as well as variety of forms; from Moses Harris, *An Exposition of English Insects . . .* (1782).

about the side-effects of human military and industrial developments, and his work on fruit-fly mutations, themselves produced an interesting side effect in the late 1950s explosion of films about insects who mutate into alarming (usually giant or lethal) forms as a result of exposure to radiation. The first example of this genre is *Them!* (1954), in which nuclear tests in the New Mexico desert produce gigantic mutated ants. Three more films of this kind appeared in 1957. In *The Beginning of the End*, the heroes struggle with giant grasshoppers advancing on Chicago whose growth has been triggered by eating radioactive wheat. In *Monster from Green Hell*, scientists searching for an experimental rocket that has crashed in Africa discover that radiation from its reactor has caused its cargo of wasps to grow to enormous size. In *The Black Scorpion*, giant scorpions are among the mutated creatures produced by a nuclear blast. Interestingly, the fly makes a rather different showing in the entomological cinema of the 1950s. *The Fly* (1958), based on a story by George Langelaan, tells the story of a subtler kind of invasion. In it, a scientist who has invented a teleporter that allows him to transport inorganic and organic materials across space decides to test his device by transporting himself. He fails to notice that a house fly has entered the transportation chamber with him, with the result that he ends up selectively combined with it, with a fly's head and arm in place of his own. After his unavailing and increasingly desperate attempts to reconstitute himself, his wife assists him to commit suicide by bringing down an industrial press on his deformed head and arm.[54] In this story, the fly represents no direct threat from the outside. Rather, it seems to stand for chance, accident or noise in the system. Instead of attacking or invading humanity in a face-to-face assault that can be beaten off, the fly insinuates itself into the human form, deforming rather than destroying. As so often, the fly is a proximate enemy.

Return of the Fly: the poster for the 1959 sequel to *The Fly*, in which the scientist's son renews his matter-transporting experiments, with similar results.

From the 1930s onwards the attention of geneticists had shifted to effects at a molecular level, and *Drosophila*, though it remained a staple of genetic research, lost its kingpin position. But then, in the 1970s, a new use emerged for the fruit fly. Once again, mutation was at the centre of things. But where research earlier in the century had concentrated on how mutations were inherited and distributed through a population, biologists now began to wonder about the processes whereby a mutation comes about, as a means to understand normal processes of development. The focus thus shifted from reproduction to embryology. Once again, the fruit fly's speed of development was a strong recommendation, for it develops from fertilized egg to embryo within nine days. As François Jacob neatly puts it, 'The old question, how does heredity function in the fruit fly? was replaced by the question, how is a fruit fly built?'[55]

From embodying the force of capricious chance, the fly 'thus became a sort of ideal model. Whatever progress we are able to make today in the genetic study of mice or humans, we owe to the fly.'[56] Far from constituting noise in the system, the fly could now be constituted as representative of all living forms, in its capacity to hold back the drift of energy into formlessness:

> The blowfly (*Phormia regina*) like all species of life, is a temporary form, through which flow energy and matter, the matter becoming, for a while, fly, and then passing on. The fly is just another way to reverse entropy in this planet, to defy, apparently, the Second Law of Thermodynamics. It is another way to build orderly complexity, in a system characterized by increasing disorder and randomness.[57]

A blow fly seen from below.

Such thoughts have allowed geneticists to challenge the claim regularly made by medieval theologians following St Augustine that nobody but God could make a fly. Genetic experimentation has certainly shown biologists much about the processes needed to unmake a fly, and the first stage in the opposite process of making a fly was achieved with the sequencing of almost all the genes in *Drosophila melanogaster* in March 2000.[58]

It is not surprising that some of the most recurrent themes in fruit-fly research should revert to the traditional ways in which humans and flies are related. Perhaps most prominent in this is the question of time. Humans have traditionally employed flies to remind them that time flies. Genetic research seems to confirm that *Drosophilae* are indeed, in Timon of Athens's contemptuous phrase, 'time's flies' (*Timon of Athens*, III. 6, 53). It has long been known that the activities of flies are closely tied to cyclical patterns, especially of light. Vincent Dethier describes the alarm of his cleaning lady when he told her that his flies had informed him of her late arrival. In fact, she had regularly induced a spike in the laboratory flies' activity graph by switching on the lights on her arrival at 8.00 every evening.[59] It has been thought for a long time that these cycles of activity are controlled by a single command clock in the brain, but recent work has begun to suggest that fruit flies may actually have timing devices spread throughout their bodies. Experiments at the University of Texas revealed that olfactory sensitivity in fruit flies became more intense at night, because of the presence in the fly's antennae of a trio of proteins known to mark time in the brain. When the flies were genetically altered to remove these peripheral proteins, the daily fluctuations in the sense of smell disappeared. That the fruit fly should be a creature that ticks throughout its anatomy suggests the possibility of finding similar multiple chronometric mechanisms in other organisms, including humans.[60]

But the fruit-fly research that has attracted most attention in recent years has been concerned not with the rhythm but with the duration of the fly's life. The fly focuses ideas about temporal, as well as spatial extension. The fly is often thought of emblematically as the creature of a day. This is why hangers-on and followers of fashion are often referred to as 'flies', as in Timon's condemnation of 'fools of fortune, trencher-friends, time's flies,/Cap and knee slaves, vapours, and minute-jacks!' (*Timon of Athens*, III. 6, 53–7). Aelian wrote of a fly he called the *ephemeron*, or 'day-fly', from the Greek meaning 'living for one day'. Aristotle had given this name to the water-breeding insect also known as the mayfly or shad-fly, but Aelian seems to have confused it with *Drosophila*, the fruit fly or 'vinegar-fly'.[61] 'They are generated in wine', he writes, and 'when the vessel is opened they fly out, see the light, and die.' Where some have used the fly to point up lessons regarding the brevity of all mortal existence, Aelian finds consolation in the fact that such flies do not live long enough to meet with suffering: 'Thus it is that Nature has permitted them to come to life, but has rescued them as soon as possible from life's evils, so that they are neither aware of their own misfortune nor are spectators of the misfortune of others.'[62]

Michael Rose of the University of California at Irvine has selectively bred flies that live for 130 days rather than the 40 that is usual for fruit flies.[63] In 1998 Seymour Benzer at the California Institute of Technology discovered flies with a mutation that enabled them to live for 35 per cent longer than normal: they named it the Methuselah gene.[64] Even more surprising is the fact that the greybeard flies seem also to be fitter than flies of normal longevity, flying up to five times faster and resisting conditions of stress and deprivation much better. However, there is a cost. It appears that the Methuselah flies are not able to maintain such high rates of fertility as ordinary wild flies.

Many flies employ characteristic patterns of flight and wing vibration in their mating rituals. This photograph shows the courting dance of the bee-mimicking 'drone fly' *Eristalis*, in which the male hovers over the female as she rests on a flower-head.

Indeed, work at University College, London, has suggested that one of the most important factors in shortening the lives of flies is mating or, more specifically, the stress of the elaborate courting ritual, which for *Drosophila* involves vibrating one wing at a time at a very particular frequency.

In 1986 David Cronenberg produced a remake of Kurt Neumann's film *The Fly* (1958). The film adds some telling new features to the story. The most important of these is that the scientist, Seth Brundle, and the fly do not exchange particular parts of their body, a head and an arm, but are merged at the level of the genetic code. Thus Brundle does not step out of the transporter with any fly-like mutations but the hybrid 'Brundle-Fly' that he has become slowly develops fly characteristics: tough insect-like hairs, huge strength, inexhaustible energy, insatiable sexual hunger and a craving for sweetness. The spatial rearrangement brought about in Langelaan's story and reproduced in the 1958 film adaptation of it thus becomes a temporal convergence in Cronenberg's version. As he explained in an interview, the aim was not to show a werewolf-like metamorphosis, in which the form of the wolf emerges from that of the man, but rather a merging:

> The primary image and one of the things that the producers and I spoke about and wanted to avoid was having Brundle turn into a 185-pound fly. It would be silly if Brundle was just turning into this huge fly, and physiologically impossible, even given the fantasy elements of any sci-fi horror film. It would have been as silly as the head switch in the original, and it wouldn't even work as well as that since this isn't the '50s anymore. I wanted to make sure, as Brundle says, that he was evolving into something that had never existed before, a real fusion between an insect and a man that would embody elements of both.[65]

The fly had another advantage for Cronenberg, in that it is associated with decomposition. One of the most memorable moments in the film shows Seth Brundle vomiting copiously over a chocolate bar to dissolve it before eating. Although Brundle develops characteristics of the adult fly – bristles, the capacity to walk on ceilings – he never seems to be coming close to developing wings or the powers of flight. Cronenberg seems more interested in the incipient, indeterminate state of the maggot. Asked

Seth Brundle shows the effects of his molecular mingling with a house fly in David Cronenberg's *The Fly* of 1986. Brundle is telling his girlfriend 'I'm an insect who dreamt he was a man, and loved it. But now the dream is over, and the insect is awake.'

repeatedly if the film had reference to the AIDS epidemic that was growing so rapidly at the time, Cronenberg replied that the transformations in the film had to do with another much more familiar experience. They are, he said, a metaphor for ageing.[66] And yet Brundle is one of a sequence of Cronenberg characters who begin to experience horrifying transformation as a positive experience, or at least as one to be explored. Where the scientist's narrative in the 1958 version of *The Fly* points up the conventional lesson that science should not meddle with forces beyond its control, Cronenberg's own comments about the film echo those of his scientist-character, who is determined to explore his new condition. 'I deal with that . . . in *The Fly*. The idea of a creative cancer; something that you would normally see as a disease now goes to another level of creativity and starts sculpting with your own body.'[67]

Four years later a novel appeared that was to speculate about another, even more far-reaching, way in which the fly might be implicated in the making and remaking of life. Michael Crichton's *Jurassic Park* (1990) develops the supposition that ancient dinosaur DNA recovered from the gut of a prehistoric mosquito trapped in amber might allow dinosaurs themselves

Long-legged fly of the *Dolichopodidae* family.

Fossil sand fly in amber, of the sub-family *Phlebotominae*.

to be cloned and brought back to life.[68] Crichton had got the idea for the novel from the work of palaeontologists George and Roberta Poinar, who in 1976 had begun looking to see whether amber might preserve not just the outward form of insects but also the fine detail of their tissue, even down to the cellular structure. After many years spent working on nematode worms their breakthrough came in 1980 when, looking through their samples of Baltic amber, they spotted what seemed like an almost perfectly preserved mycetophilid fly. On examination, they discovered that its cells were preserved in astonishing detail. The amber had acted in ways that anticipated the methods of fixation and dehydration employed in electron microscopy, sugars in the tree sap combining with water to dehydrate and preserve the tissue in a kind of mummification.[69] The Baltic amber fly made it possible to ask the question: if tissues were so well preserved, might DNA also have been preserved? When fossils of biting flies were found in Cretaceous amber in Alberta in 1993, the possibility suggested itself that they might contain some dinosaur DNA.[70] In the summer of 1993 the Poinars were able to announce the discovery of preserved DNA strands more than 125 million years old.

The 60-million-year-old microfossil of a fly.

By the end of the twentieth century, no other creature seemed so fit for the purpose of communicating between ideas of form, decomposition and recomposition as the fly. It is the fact that flies so insistently raise these questions of form, purpose, mutability and making that makes a zoopoetics of the fly so pregnant and, as we will see in the final chapter, seems to give the fly a role in its own cultural making, as a signal emerging from the background noise.

A robber-fly (family *Asilidae*) from the Oligocene period (38-23 million years ago), fossilized in shale from Idaho.

7 Fly Leaves

Thinking about flies is complicated by the fact that flies are often a recourse for thinking about thought, or at least its disordering. This is perhaps because, as tenants of the air, flies are implicated in the mind's favoured image of itself and its own airy actions. Perhaps one might see the angel, the incorporeal embodiment of the thought of God, as an image of thought in its fullest and most infinitive form. The angel represents the promise of a soaring, expansive, ascensional thought utterly unconstrained by matter, space and time, a thought that arises and subsists in its self-surpassing. As so often, the fly is the opposite to the angel. Flies buzzing around one's head are at once a distraction to thought and an image of thought distracted, pulverized and pulled apart. The association of the fly with decomposition perhaps helps motivate this association with distraction and madness. The visitations of the gadfly were well known among the Greeks and Romans to produce fits of desperate fury in oxen and cattle. Virgil describes its effect on herds: 'Fierce it is, and sharp of note; before it whole herds scatter in terror through the woods: with their bellowings the air is stunned and maddened.'[1] The Greek word for the gadfly, *oestrus*, came to be applied to such temporary fits of raving madness in human beings. The myth of Io, as set out in Aeschylus' *Prometheus Bound* and Ovid's *Metamorphoses*, also makes the link with the gadfly and distraction. Io is turned by her lover Zeus into a white heifer, which his jealous wife Hera demands from him, and appoints many-eyed Argus to guard. When Zeus frees her by sending Hermes to kill Argus, Hera summons up a fury in the form of a gadfly, whose stings drive her, nearly insane with torment, across Europe to Egypt. Her wanderings leave their trace in the names of the Ionian Sea and the Bosphorus ('cow's crossing').

Maggots have the same power to cause extreme disordering of the wits. The Emperor Titus, the sacker of Jerusalem, was believed to have been tormented by a biting fly that had bored into his brain; after it had eventually killed him, his skull was opened to reveal a fly the size of a pigeon. A similar story is found in Arabic sources concerning Nimrod, who was promised a 1,000-year dominion over the earth. After 300 years, he started to be tormented by a fly in his brain; he retained his human faculties for 400 years, but spent the last 300 years of his life in intellectual twilight.[2] In the version of the story given in the *Tales of the Prophets* by the twelfth-century writer Al-Kisa'i, God employs the

'Beast-fly' or *oestrus*, illustrated in Moffett's *The Theater of Insects*. Flies of the family *Oestridae*, commonly known as bot flies and in earlier times as gadflies, are parasites of horses, deer and cattle. *Oestrus ovis* or sheep bot fly deposits its young in the nasal cavities of sheep.

ARIES AND MUSCA BOREALIS.

A sky-map of 1825 shows 'Musca', a constellation of the Southern Hemisphere, first described by Europeans during a Dutch expedition to the East Indies in 1595. Here the constellation is shown tormenting a sheep (*Aries*).

services of a gnat to effect the final defeat of the tyrannous and atheistic Nimrod after his long persecution of the prophet Abraham. The gnat crawls up Nimrod's nostril to his brain, where it starts to gnaw agonizingly. The only way for Nimrod to obtain relief is to have his retainers beat his head with an iron bar, which causes the stunned gnat temporarily to leave off its chewing. One day, one of his viziers overdoes the tough love, and splits his skull in two, whereupon 'the gnat emerges like a chick from an egg, saying "There is no God but God; Abraham is the apostle of God and His Friend."'[3]

Proverbial expressions in many languages preserve this sense that to be mad is to be besieged by flies in the head: the French *avoir une tête emmouquée* means to be crazy or distracted. Flies therefore seem closely allied to dream or madness: Shelley refers to 'busy dreams, as thick as summer flies', while Keats evokes the bewildering thoughts 'born of atomies/That buzz about our slumbers, like brain-flies,/Leaving us fancy-sick'.[4] In England, madness or intemperate fancy was proverbially attributed to the internal operation of maggots rather than of flies. From the seventeenth century to the end of the nineteenth, maggots referred not just to insect larvae, but also to unpredictable fancies. To be governed by a maggot is to be in the grip of an uncontrollable obsession or delusion; to be 'maggot-pated' is to teem with such fantastical whims or caprices; and to do something 'when the maggot bites', is to be driven to it by an urgent, irrational impulse. The speaker in Robert Lloyd's poem 'Genius, Envy and Time' reassures Genius that he need take no account of transient reactions born of envy, which will subside into 'Mere excremental maggots, bred/In poet's topsy-turvy head,/Born like a momentary fly,/To flutter, buzz about, and die'.[5]

The biting of the maggot of whim or madness was often associated with the effects of ungoverned reading. The extravagant fantasies of Don Quixote drew the following judgement from Edward Ward in his English rendering of Cervantes' tale:

Idle-Tales, adorned with Wit,
And hurtful Books with cunning writ,
In shallow Brains strange Maggots breed,
And make Men Act the things they read.[6]

Novelists were blamed for spreading infestations of fancy, too. William Cowper concludes a passage of fierce derision directed at the inflammatory powers of novelists by wishing that 'a verse had power, and could command/Far, far away these fleshflies of the land,/Who fasten without mercy on the fair,/And suck, and leave a craving maggot there'.[7] The correlative itch to write also had something of the maggot in it. Samuel Wesley published in 1685 a book of poems entitled *Maggots; or, Poems on Several Subjects, Never Before Handled*, which opens with the lines 'The Maggot Bites, I must begin:/Muse! pray be civil! Enter in!/Ransack my addled pate with Care/And muster all the Maggots there!'[8]

As far as I can see, and, to nobody's very great astonishment I am sure, there are only a small number of genres of fly-writing, almost all of which we have met already in this book. There is the fly-idyll, instanced in a poem like Edmund Spenser's 'Muipotmos', which celebrates the careless life of the fly. There are also, as we have seen, mock-heroic celebrations of the fly, most famously in the poem 'Culex' traditionally attributed to Virgil, and rendered into English by Spenser (1591), in which a gnat stings a sleeping shepherd to warn him of the approach of a snake, but is then itself carelessly killed. After the gnat appears reproachfully to the shepherd in a dream, he raises a monument to it. There are also fabular uses, to point up lessons about getting above one's station or allowing oneself to be swallowed up

in idle pleasures. And there is the love-poem, or poem of dipterous seduction and lament, in which the fly offers mediated or imaginary access to the desired body of the lover (Romeo's speech about the 'carrion flies' who traffic so freely with Juliet's hands and lips belongs to this genre, and John Donne's 'The Flea' is a sophisticated variant of it).

Over the last century or so, a new subgenre of fly-writing has emerged, distinct from these pastoral, pedagogic and passional modes. The tendency to see flies as an image of thought preying upon and discomposing itself finds its expression in a mode of writing we may, with full allowance of hyperbole, name 'autodipteropoesis', in which the fly is implicated reflexively in the work of its own poetic making. For the meaning of the fly is distraction, insignificance. Indeed, a fly – well, a butterfly – is strongly implicated in our contemporary thinking about insignificance, in the form of the Lorenz effect. This describes the very sensitive dependence of complex systems on initial conditions, such that tiny and apparently insignificant variations can produce large-scale changes in state over time. The example always given comes from the title of a paper that Edward Lorenz gave to the American Association for the Advancement of Science in 1972, in which he asked: 'Does the Flap of a Butterfly's Wings in Brazil set off a Tornado in Texas?'[9] In an earlier version of the talk given in 1963, it had been a seagull's wings that had provided the rhetorical question. The replacement of the seagull by the butterfly was suggested by the butterfly-like shape of a graphical representation of dramatic divergences caused by the amplification of small variables. Perhaps in the intervening time, Lorenz had also come across the Ray Bradbury story, 'A Sound of Thunder', in which time-travelling tourists manage to effect drastic alterations in the future by crushing a single butterfly in the primeval past.[10]

Felix Boisselier, *The Shepherd*, 1808, oil on canvas. Boisselier's painting shows a repentant shepherd weeping over the tomb he has erected for the gnat who saved his life. Boisselier's monument quotes Virgil: PARVE CVLEX, PECVDVM CVSTOS / TIBI TALE MERENTI / FVNERIS OFFICIVM VITÆ PRO MVNERE REDDIT. (To thee, small gnat, in lieu of his life saved / The shepherd hath thy death's record engraved.)

When *The Simpsons* brought the two together in a parody of the Bradbury story, the butterfly underwent a further move down the scale of insignificance. Finding himself back in the primeval past as a result of jamming a fork in a broken toaster, Homer Simpson reminds himself and his audience of the narrative rules: 'As long as I stand perfectly still and don't touch anything, I won't destroy the future.' Instantly a giant mosquito dives in, prompting the inevitable response from Homer: 'Stupid bug! You go squish now!', followed by his apprehensive query: 'But that was just one little insignificant mosquito. That can't change the future, right?' (It does.)

Much of the irritation of the fly comes from the noise it makes, which seems like the opposite of meaningful speech. Indeed, many languages reproduce that buzz in the creature's name. Where Teutonic languages derive the name of the fly from the nature of its movement – English *fly*, German *Fliege* – Romance languages derive the fly's name from the sound it makes. The Greek *muia*, an imitation of the fly's buzz (or, more precisely perhaps, the hum that Greek seems to hear), gives us Latin *musca*, Italian *mosca* and Spanish *mosquito*, 'little fly', and French *mouche*. The delightful *zinzala*, for a gnat, is also found in Late Latin.[11] The fly is heard in English only in the word 'midge' which is a diminutive derived from *musca* via German *mücke*, a gnat, and yields further diminutives like 'midget', 'smidgin' and others. The sonic principle is particularly strong in the names for the fly in many Middle Eastern languages. Hebrew *zebub* (pronounced 'zvuv'), is surely one of the most magically exact onomatopoeias in any language.

From ancient to early modern times, there has been busy conjecture about the ways in which this sound was produced. Aristotle wrote that insects 'have no voice and no language, but they can emit sound by internal air or wind, though not by the emission of air or wind; for no insects are capable of respiration'.[12] The inferiority of the buzz compared to the articulate sounds produced by other animals seems to be a function of this belief that insects did not breathe, and did not produce sound from the mouth, the seat of spirit and intelligence. The fly's buzz is not articulated air, given form by the finer and more eminent air that soul was thought to be, but mere, mindless agitation. Aristophanes mocks the microscopic attentiveness of scholarship in *The Clouds*, in which a pupil of Socrates recapitulates his master's acoustic proof that the fly sings through its anus rather than its proboscis, thereby providing an ironic image of the midget musings of the philosopher.[13] Paraphrasing Aristotle's view, and seemingly modifying it slightly in the process, Thomas Browne said that the fly's buzz was made 'by the illision of an inward spirit upon a pellicle or little membrane about the precinct or pectoral division of their body'.[14] As late as 1817, William Kirby and William Spence were still declaring that 'no insect, like the larger animals, uses its mouth for utterance of any kind: in this respect they are all perfectly mute; and though incessantly noisy, are everlastingly silent'.[15] The humming or buzzing that has furnished the fly's name in so many parts of Europe is therefore an accidental rather than essential feature of it, in keeping with the belief in the fly's anyway supererogatory nature. The nineteenth-century historian of religion Thomas Inman suggested that the Hebrew word *-zabab* in the name of Beelzebub should be understand to signify murmur, hum or buzz, rather than flies, and connects the name with the priestly practice of creeping underneath a statue to murmur or mutter indistinct responses. If this explanation convinces, Beelzebub might mean 'My Lord who murmurs'.[16] Lucian tells a story of a young girl called Muia, who gave her name to the fly. Pretty, vivacious, but garrulous, she incurred

An 1850s cross-section of a house fly, showing the 'pectoral division' that Thomas Browne thought produced the insect's buzz.

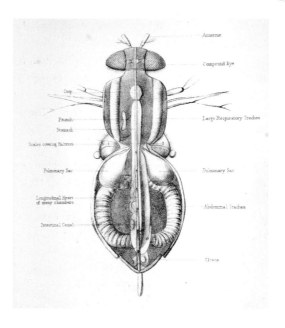

Antennæ

Compound Eye

Crop

Large Respiratory Trachea

Paunch

Stomach

Scales covering Halteres

Pulmonary Sac

Pulmonary Sac

Longitudinal Heart of many chambers

Abdominal Trachea

Intestinal Canal

Cloaca

the wrath of Selene by becoming a rival for the love of Endymion. As a punishment for continually waking him from his sleep with her chatter, Muia was turned into a creature able to do nothing more than repeat her name, even, one might almost say, be nothing more than her vacuously but distractingly self-designating name.[17] This story exists in other cultures, which have a similarly disparaging view of the fly's sound. In a Nigerian folk tale, a black fly named Njinn-I-Nyakk causes a boy in a tree to drop a knife by her buzzing, unleashing a chain of consequences that results in the guinea fowl weeping over her broken eggs and neglecting her duty of waking the dawn with her cry. Obassi, lord of creation, asks all the creatures in turn how this has come about. Only the fly will give no reply, but simply buzzes: so, as a punishment, Obassi commands him 'to remain speechless for evermore, and to do nothing but buzz about and be present wherever a foul thing lies'.[18]

Buzzing has come to mean indistinguishable, inarticulate sound, the very sound of non-meaning. The word seems to have arisen in the sixteenth century, and early on came to be applied, not just literally to the sounds of bees and flies, but also to indistinct human speech. Thus Hamlet's insulting 'Buzz, buzz!' (*Hamlet*, II. 2, 281) to Polonius indicates a sound that is mere vacant noise. The word is also commonly used to indicate rumour, as in Francis Quarles's reference to 'bruit and buzz'd Opinion',[19] or irritating triviality, as in the character who complains in 1694: 'I am quite sick of the Common Buz at Coffee-Houses, News frequently false, mostly uncertain, and sometimes absurdly Ridiculous'.[20] In his popular poem *Night Thoughts* Edward Young similarly regrets the foolish chase after 'The momentary buzz of vain renown,/A name, a mortal immortality'.[21] The more contemporary term 'buzz-word' still suggests both the excitement of the nonce, and the numb vacuity of a cliché; while, in computing, a programme that is 'buzzing' is one that seems to be running with no sign of progress or prospect of finishing.[22]

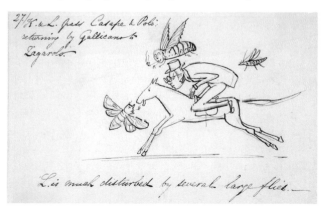

Edward Lear, on his travels through Italy, found himself 'much disturbed by several large flies', as recorded in his ink drawing of 1842.

Others have found more music in the sound of the fly. Alberti remarks on the plaintiveness of the sound of the fly trapped in a web, and suggests that Pythagoras may have meant a homage to the fly's Greek name in the word 'music' (it is said that Muia was the name of the daughter of Pythagoras).[23] Others have felt that the very lowliness and insignificance of the fly's buzz make it apt to become charged with significance. In the course of an 'Essay on the Sublimity and Beauty of Sound', Archibald Alison, an eighteenth-century writer on aesthetics, considered that '[t]here is scarcely in nature a more trifling Sound than the buzz of Flies, yet I believe there is no man of common Taste, who, in the deep silence of a summer's noon, has not found something strikingly sublime in this inconsiderable sound'.[24] Keats perhaps registers something of this sublimity in his 'Ode to a Nightingale', in the mesmerizing sound that emanates from the musk rose, 'the murmurous haunt of flies on summer eves'.[25] He treats the buzzing of gnats with equivalent solemnity in 'To Autumn', in which 'in a wailful choir, the small gnats mourn'.[26] Perhaps the greatest counter to evocations of the nuisance and distraction of flies is to be found in *Swann's Way*, the first volume of Proust's *Remembrance of Things Past*. The narrator Marcel remembers lying on his bed on hot summer afternoons, with the shutters drawn to preserve the coolness of the room. The splendour and glory of the day are apprehensible only in the sunlight that seems poised between the shutters and the glass, 'like a butterfly poised upon a flower', and, more importantly, the 'resonant atmosphere' supplied by

> the flies who performed for my benefit, in their tiny chorus, as it were the chamber music of summer, evoking it quite differently from a snatch of human music which, heard by chance in high summer, will remind you of it

later, whereas the music of the flies is bound to the season by a more compelling tie – born of the sunny days, and not to be reborn but with them, containing something of their essential nature, it not merely calls up their image in our memory, but guarantees their return, their actual, circumjacent, immediately accessible presence.[27]

Proust's great novel is built around such moments, in which the past is not simply recollected but resurrected. Though fewer readers remember the hum of the flies than the madeleine, its power to preserve and restore the essence of the past is central to the book. Flies are rarely so much of the essence of things as here.

Perhaps the subtlest and most disconcerting treatment of the fly's signature noise is Emily Dickinson's poem 'I heard a Fly buzz'. The poem evokes the moment of awed pause before the speaker's own death. Everything seems in place for the solemn event of her passing, with grief duly vented ('The Eyes around – had wrung them dry – '), and worldly effects prudently disposed of ('I willed my Keepsakes – Signed away/What portion of me be/Assignable'). The suspense is 'like the Stillness in the Air – /Between the Heaves of Storm'. Into this solemn intermission absurdly blunders a fly:

and then it was
There interposed a Fly –

With Blue – uncertain stumbling Buzz –
Between the light – and me –
And then the Windows failed – and then
I could not see to see – [28]

Perhaps the speaker has indeed removed to death, in the steady and inexorable sequence promised by the poem, with its 'and then . . . and then'. If so, perhaps the speaker can no longer 'see to see' because she has moved beyond mere seeing, the fly being the herald of a vision so exalted that it is no longer a question of seeing anything as mundane as light, windows or insects. But something seems wrong with this hypothesis. For the fly's buzz is no decisive, annunciatory trump, but something uncertain, stumbling. Far from unveiling the Light, it comes 'Between the light – and me'. Perhaps what the fly announces is in fact a postponement of revelation, a purgatorial withdrawal of the light by which revelation might reveal itself, leaving the speaker suspended somewhere between that light and where she is, just as the fly is. It is Dickinson's Cronenberg moment, in which the fly comes between the thinker and her thinking. As the principle of noise, irrelevance, interruption, the fly gets into the works, innocently but sinisterly going to work on the workings of the poem. Just as the vital spirits are dispersed at the crucial moment of the conception of the young Tristram Shandy by an unexpectedly mundane question from Mrs S, preventing him from ever properly adding up to his life, so the consummation of death is interrupted by the fly.

Ambrose Bierce teasingly proposes a constitutive role for flies in the history of writing. Punctuation, he claims, was unknown among the earliest writers in most languages, who 'never punctuated at all, but worked right along free-handed, without that abruption of the thought which comes from the use of points'.[29] Punctuation, he informs the reader with mock-scholarly solemnity, arises from the attentions of flies to the writers' manuscripts and, in particular, the dots of faeces they leave on the paper in random commentary:

The flies illustrating Moffett's *The Theater of Insects* appear both to besmirch and adorn the page in the expressive way noted by Ambrose Bierce.

These creatures, which have always been distinguished for a neighborly and companionable familiarity with authors, liberally or niggardly embellish the manuscripts in process of growth under the pen, according to their bodily habit, bringing out the sense of the work by a species of interpretation superior to, and independent of, the writer's powers . . . In the work of these primitive scribes all the punctuation is found, by the modern investigator with his optical instruments and chemical tests, to have been inserted by the writers' ingenious and serviceable collaborator, the common house-fly – *Musca maledicta*.[30]

The formative – or deforming – role of flies in the etiology of texts might almost be taken as an image of the work of Bierce's own cod-lexicographic enterprise, which offers impish irrelevance in place of revelation and allows misprision to interrupt the smooth transmission of truth. Perhaps his definition is suggested in part by the fact that from the late seventeenth century to the mid-nineteenth a printer's devil was referred to as a 'fly' (this probably being suggested by the fact that a fly was also the name for a demonic familiar).[31] Bierce concludes this entry by recommending to contemporary critics the decorative enhancement of sense offered by these anonymous flying scribes:

Fully to understand the important services that flies perform to literature it is only necessary to lay a page of some popular novelist alongside a saucer of cream-and-molasses in a sunny room and observe 'how the wit brightens and the style refines' in accurate proportion to the duration of exposure.[32]

Jacopo de' Barbari,
*Portrait of Luca
Pacioli*, 1495,
oil on wood.

This is not the last time that Bierce links flies and literature in his *Devil's Dictionary*. His entry under 'tzetze (or tsetse) fly' reads 'An African insect (*Glossina morsitans*) whose bite is commonly regarded as nature's most efficacious remedy for insomnia, though some patients prefer that of the American novelist (*Mendax interminabilis*)'.[33]

Heidegger writes of the animal that it is 'poor in world', by which he means that the animal, a lizard on a stone, for example, is not able to recognize or have a relation to the stone, or the world 'as such'. Only human beings, he suggests, have the capacity to open, illuminate or allow the beings of things in their being.[34] This is precisely what flies withhold. In our enforced intimacy with flies, we do not get being back. This is not in the least because flies have it in for us. That would be company of sorts, since the enmity of flies would be a way of forcing them into a coherently symmetrical relationship of antagonism with us. It is rather because we are not in the picture for them. This is perhaps the real meaning of the reference to the fly in the 'fly-on-the-wall' documentary. It is not just that the witness is unobserved by us; it is also that the fly does not actively or consciously observe us, in the sense that it does not watch us as we might expect a human eye to watch us. The claim made by such documentaries is that they show reality watching, without looking at, itself. What we see in the fly is ourselves unseen by it; we are needled and made uneasy by our insignificance to this most definitionally insignificant creature. This is what we most need to extirpate, this stubborn disinclination to make us out, or keep us in focus as anything more than our mortality, our blood, sweat and tears, our droppings, the precocious stinks that slink from us. It is precisely the fact that we do not figure for the fly except as 'A Flash; A minute;/A painted Toombe, with putrifaction in it', that the fly can be so much our intimate, our familiar.[35]

Sometimes we will borrow or hitchhike on flies' sensory capacities, as in the case of the truffle fly, or *Sullia gigantae*, a straw-coloured fly that performs a distinctive, springing dance over the soil around the base of oak trees where it will lay its eggs and in which the odoriferous fungi can be found. Nowadays we more usually farm flies for genes and genetic knowledge. As we saw in the opening chapter, flies have long farmed us for our excrements (no civilization ever rose without increasing and concentrating its droppings; no order without ordure). Flies and humans are asymmetrically deterritorializing. Flies are the noise that muffles, confuses, meddles with clear thinking, dirties up our social signals, just as we perhaps are a kind of noise in the fly's system. Flies and humans are each other's parasite or interference. Each gives the other its unbeing.

The lives of humans and flies have intertwined in deep and complex ways. Robert E. Kohler has argued against the assumption that flies are merely the object of human attention, or the cause of their distraction. The fruit flies of genetics are

> active players in the relationship with experimental biologists, capable of unexpectedly changing the rules of experimental practice . . . We need to see the relation between Drosophila and drosophilists as an interactive and evolving symbiosis within the special ecological spaces of experimental laboratories.[36]

But if flies and humans form a symbiosis, what is its purpose or outcome? The intimate, intermittent aggregations we form with flies and they with us is never proportionate, never rounds off or adds up, is never quite in focus or to scale. There is no seeing eye-to-eye with a fly, nor ever a milieu of the as-such in which flies and humans might face up to each other. And yet, for humans, there is also no disposing of or dispensing with flies. Between flies and humans, there can only ever be a haunted, interrupted truce. Charles Bukowski's poem '2 flies' describes the maddeningly unintelligible dance of two 'angry bits of life' in the room as he is trying to read. He succeeds in killing one of them, but is left unsettled, perplexed, implicated:

> something has happened,
> something has soiled my
> day,
> sometimes it does not

take a man
or a woman,
only something alive;
I sit and watch
the small one;
we are woven together
in the air
and the living;
it is late
for both of us [37]

In seeking to make something of the fly, whether through mechanical artifice, genetic engineering or poetic composition, we simultaneously draw nearer to the understanding of our own make-up. Perhaps the fly may yet impart to us not just the secrets of our biological nature, but also new modes of attention. Michel Serres has adopted the flight of the fly as a kind of motif for the abrupt, unexpected, diagonal transitions of mind required to make sense of a complex world: 'Speed is the elegance of thought, which mocks stupidity, heavy and slow. Intelligence thinks and says the unexpected; it moves with the fly, with its flight.'[38] From signifying death, decay and the *horror vacui*, flies have increasingly come to seem not just as affording oblique and accidental insights into the nature of things, but as the zigzagging but royal road to the understanding of how things come, and cease, to be.

What could it mean to be 'face-to-face' with a fly?

184

Timeline of the Fly

c. 230 million years BC	*c.* 141 BC – AD 224	43 BC	AD 107
(Middle Triassic period) First fossil records of flies 	The *Vendîdâd*, a compilation of religious laws and mythical tales forming part of the Zoroastrian *Zend-Avesta*, gives detailed instructions for driving away the Drug Nasu, or fly-demon	Virgil said to have constructed a brass fly that kept Naples free of flies for eight years	The first recorded case of opthalmomyiasis: Tu Ken in China, who became infected with maggots in his eyes when feigning death by lying outside the city walls

c. 1460	1602	1688	1665	1751
Johann Müller (1436–1476), astronomer, is said to have constructed an iron fly in his laboratories in Nuremberg	Ulisse Aldrovandi offers a lengthy description of different kinds of fly in *De animalibus insectis*, the first systematic work of entomology	Francesco Redi demonstrates that flies are not bred spontaneously from decaying meat	Robert Hooke uses a microscope to describe and draw the eye and foot of a fly in *Micrographia* 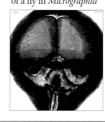	Abbé Nicholas Louis de Lacaille names the constellation *Musca Australis*, the Southern Fly, now known simply as *Musca*

1910	1928	1958
After two years working with *Drosophila melanogaster*, Thomas Hunt Morgan of Columbia University succeeds in breeding from a mutant fly with white rather than red eyes, inaugurating modern genetics	Following his observations during the First World War of the beneficial effects of wound-infestation by fly maggots, William Baer successfully treats two children for osteomyelitis with maggots	Release of *The Fly*, a film directed by Kurt Neumann and based on George Langelaan's story 

c. AD 150	*c.* AD 200	1247	1285	1441–3
The Syrian Lucian of Samosata composes 'The Fly'	First mention of fishing with an artificial fly, in Aelian's *Natural History*	*Hsi Yuan Lu* ('The Washing Away of Wrongs') describes the first forensic use of flies when the insects drawn to invisible traces of blood identified the sickle used in a murder	In the Catalan town of Girona a swarm of flies pours out from the disturbed tomb of St Narcissus to drive away French invaders	The Florentine humanist Leon Battista Alberti composes 'Musca', modelled on Lucian's 'The Fly'

1776	1782	1799	1895
Hessian fly first appears in Staten Island and spreads rapidly across the USA	Charles De Geer describes *Empusa muscae*, the lethal fly-fungus	Dominique-Jean Larrey observes the beneficial effects of infestation by fly maggots on the healing of wounds among Napoleon's soldiers in Egypt	Bloodsucking flies of the genus *Glossina* (tsetse fly) linked conclusively to the spread of sleeping sickness by David Bruce

1978	1982	1986	1998
Christiane Nüsslein-Volhard and Eric Wieschaus begin using fruit fly mutations to map the process whereby the body of the fly is formed	George and Roberta Poinar discover an almost perfectly preserved mycetophilid fly in Baltic amber	David Cronenberg remakes *The Fly*	Seymour Benzer of the California Institute of Technology discovers the *methuselah* gene, which extends the life of the fruit fly by 35 per cent

References

1 FLY FAMILIAR

1 André Bay, *Des mouches et des hommes* (Paris, 1979), p. 56.
My translation.

2 John Clare, 'House or Window Flies', in *The Later Poems of John Clare: 1837–1864*, ed. Eric Robinson and David Powell (Oxford, 1984), vol. II, p. 760.

3 Pliny the Elder, *Natural History*, with an English translation by H. Rackham et al. (London, 1938–63), XXIX. 34, vol. VIII, p. 253; *Plutarch*'s *Moralia*, with an English translation by Edwin L. Minar, F. H. Sandbach and W. C. Helmbold (Cambridge, MA, and London, 1999), vol. IX, p. 171.

4 Ralph Waldo Emerson, *The Conduct of Life: The Complete Works of Ralph Waldo Emerson* (Boston, MA, and New York, 1903–4), vol. VI, p. 269.

5 Charles Olson, 'A Big Fat Fly', in *Collected Poems of Charles Olson* (Berkeley, CA, and Los Angeles, 1987), pp. 642–3.

6 Plautus, 'Mercator, or The Merchant', in *Plautus*, trans. Paul Nixon (London, 1916–), vol. III, pp. 38–41.

7 Gittin 6b, Ketuboth 77 b, Sabbat 121 b. Ludwig Lewysohn, *Die Zoologie des Talmuds: eine umfassende Darstellung der rabbinischen Zoologie, unter steter Vergleichung der Forschungen älterer und neuerer Schriftsteller* (Frankfurt am Main, 1858), p. 313.

8 Jan Knappert, *The Encylopaedia of Middle Eastern Mythology and Religion* (Shaftesbury, 1993), p. 125.

9 *The American Cyclopaedia: A Popular Dictionary of General Knowledge,*

ed. George Ripley and Charles A. Dana (New York, 1873–6), vol.
VII, p. 294.

10 William Golding, *Lord of the Flies* (London, 1996), p. 111.

11 *The Hieroglyphics of Horapollo* (I. 51), trans. George Boas
(Princeton, NJ, 1993), p. 66.

12 Robert G. Morkot, *Historical Dictionary of Ancient Egyptian
Warfare* (Lanham, MD, and Oxford, 2003), p. 4.

13 Gene Kritsky, 'Tombs, Mummies and Flies', *Bulletin of the
Entomological Association of America*, XXXI (1985), p. 19.

14 Homer, *Iliad* (2. 469), trans. A. T. Murray, rev. William F. Wyatt
(Cambridge, MA, and London, 1999), vol. I, pp. 95–7.

15 Ibid. (17. 567), vol. II, p. 271.

16 Lucian, 'The Fly', in *Lucian*, trans. A. M. Harmon (London and
New York, 1913), vol. I, p. 87.

17 Ibid., p. 93.

18 Ibid., p. 83.

19 Ibid., p. 91.

20 Leon Battista Alberti, 'Musca', in *Apologhi ed elogi*, ed. Rosario
Contarino (Genoa, 1984), p. 176. This edition is of the Latin text
with a parallel Italian translation. References hereafter in my text
and translations my own.

21 John Ruskin, *The Queen of the Air: Being a Study of the Greek Myths
of Cloud and Storm*, in *The Works of John Ruskin*, ed. E. T. Cook and
Alexander Wedderburn, (London, 1903–12), vol. XIX, p. 331.
References hereafter in text.

22 Galway Kinnell, 'The Fly', in *Three Books: Body Rags; Mortal Acts,
Mortal Words; The Past* (Boston, MA, 1993), p. 18.

23 Quoted in Bay, *Des mouches et des hommes*, p. 74.

24 *Notes and Queries*, CLXXVII (1939), p. 479.

25 Guy de Maupassant, 'La Tombe', in *Contes et nouvelles*, ed. Louis
Forestier (Paris, 1974), vol. II, p. 216. My translation.

26 *A Dictionary of Superstitions*, ed. Iona Opie and Moira Tatem
(Oxford, 1992), p. 164.

27 *The Complete Poetry and Prose of William Blake*, ed. David Erdman,
rev. edn (Berkeley and Los Angeles, 1982), pp. 23–4.

1 Sigmund Freud, 'The Uncanny', in *The Standard Edition of the Psychological Works of Sigmund Freud*, trans. James Strachey et al. (London, 1953–74), vol. XVII, pp. 222–6.

2 Marina Warner, *Fantastic Metamorphoses: Other Worlds: Ways of Telling the Self* (Oxford, 2002), pp. 90–93.

3 Edmund Spenser, 'Muipotmos', in *Poetical Works*, ed. J. C. Smith and E. de Selincourt (London, New York and Toronto, 1952), pp. 515–20.

4 Pliny the Elder, *Natural History* (XI, 43), trans. H. Rackham et al. (London, 1938–63), vol. III, p. 507; Aelian, *On The Characteristics of Animals* (II. 29), trans. A. F. Scholfield (London and Cambridge, MA, 1958–9), vol. I, p. 129.

5 Lucian, 'The Fly', in *Lucian*, trans. A. M. Harmon (London and New York, 1913), vol. I, p. 89.

6 Kemp Malone, 'Rose and Cypress', *Publications of the Modern Language Association*, XLIII (1928), p. 417.

7 R. O. Winstedt, *Shaman, Saiva and Sufi: A Study of the Evolution of Malay Magic* (London, Bombay and Sydney, 1925), p. 65.

8 Gene Kritsky, 'Tombs, Mummies and Flies', *Bulletin of the Entomological Association of America*, XXXI (1985), pp. 18–19.

9 E. A. Wallis Budge, *The Mummy: A Handbook of Egyptian Funerary Archaeology* (London and New York, 1987), p. 324.

10 Charles Bukowski, '2 Flies', in *Play the Piano Drunk Like a Percussion Instrument until the Fingers Begin To Bleed a Bit* (Santa Rosa, CA, 1979), pp. 33–4.

11 Jean Bodin, *De la Démonomanie des sorciers* (Paris, 1587), p. 246. My translation.

12 Ibid., p. 16.

13 Ibid., p. 134.

14 St Augustine, *The City of God Against the Pagans* (II. 22), trans. R. W. Dyson (Cambridge, 1998), p. 81.

15 Apuleius, *The Golden Ass; or, Metamorphoses*, trans. E. J. Kenney (Harmondsworth, 1998), p. 33.

16 John Webster, *The Displaying of Supposed Witchcraft* (London,

1677), pp. 88–9.

17 Douglas L. Penney and Michael O. Wise, 'By the Power of Beelzebub: An Aramaic Incantation Formula from Qumran (4Q560)', *Journal of Biblical Literature*, CXIII (1994), p. 634.

18 Balthasar Bekker, *The World Turn'd Upside Down; or, A Plain Detection of Errors, In the Common or Vulgar Belief, Relating To Spirits, Spectres or Ghosts, Dæmons, Witches, &c.* (London, 1700), p. 205.

19 Martin Del Rio, *Disquisitionum magicarum libri sex* (n. p., 1657), p. 351. My translation.

20 Montague Summers, *The Vampire: His Kith and Kin* (London, 1928), p. 198.

21 Richard Boulton, *A Compleat History of Magick, Sorcery and Witchcraft* (London, 1715–16), vol. I, p. 259.

22 Pierre de L'Ancre, *Tableau de l'inconstance des mauvais anges et demons* (Paris, 1613), p. 505.

23 Joseph Glanvill, *Saducismus Triumphatus; or, Full and Plain Evidence Concerning Witches and Apparitions. In Two Parts. The First Treating of their Possibility; The Second of their Real Existence*, 3rd edn (London, 1681), Part 2, pp. 144–5.

24 Kevin Crossley Holland, *The Norse Myths* (London, 1980), p. 68.

25 *Orpheus in the Underworld: Operetta in Three Acts*, trans. Geoffrey Dunn (London, 1981) [original libretto Hector Crémieux and Ludovic Halévy], p. 48.

26 Laurent Bordelon, *A History of the Ridiculous Extravagancies of Monsieur Oufle; Occasion'd by his Reading Books Treating of Magick* (London, 1711), p. 98.

27 Ibid.

28 Ibid., pp. 218–19.

29 E.C.B. Maclaurin, 'Beelzeboul', *Novum Testamentum*, XX (1978), pp. 156–60.

30 Charles Fontinoy, 'Les noms du Diable et leur étymologie', in *Orientalia: J. Duschene-Guillemin Emerito Oblata* (Leiden, 1984), pp. 164–6.

31 *The Book of the Sacred Magic of Abramelin the Mage, as Delivered by*

Abraham the Jew unto his Son Lamech, AD 1458, trans. S. L. Macgregor Mathers (London, 1900), p. 110.

32 'The Testament of Solomon', trans. F. C. Conybeare, *Jewish Quarterly Review*, XI (1898), pp. 19, 21–2; D. C. Duling, 'The Testament of Solomon', in *The Old Testament Pseudepigrapha*, ed. J. H. Charlesworth (New York, 1983), pp. 935–59.

33 Pliny, *Natural History* (x. 40), vol. III, p. 341.

34 Pausanias, *Description of Greece* (v. 14), trans. W.H.S. Jones and H. A. Ormerod (Cambridge, MA, and London, 1954–71), vol. II, pp. 457–9.

35 St Jerome, 'To Marcella', Letter 44, in *Letters and Select Works*, trans. W. H. Freemantle, *Select Library of Nicene and Post-Nicene Fathers of the Christian Church*. Second series, vol. VI (Oxford and New York, 1893), p. 58.

36 *The Questions of King Milinda*, trans. T. W. Rhys Davids (Oxford, 1894), Part II, p. 351.

37 John Shefferius [John Scheffer], *The History of Lapland: Wherein Are Shewed the Original Manners, Habits, Marriages, Conjurations, &c. of That People* (Oxford, 1674), p. 59.

38 *The Zend-Avesta. Part I: The Vendîdâd*, trans. James Darmesteter (Delhi, 1995), p. 75

39 Ibid., pp. 109–10.

40 Robert Means Lawrence, *The Magic of the Horse-Shoe: With Other Folk-Lore Notes* (London, 1898), p. 291.

41 J. Desnoyer, 'L'Excommunication des insectes et d'autres animaux nuisibles', *Bulletin de Comité Historique des Monuments Ecrits de L'Histoire de France*, IV (1853), pp. 36–54; E. P. Evans, *The Criminal Prosecution and Capital Punishment of Animals* (London, 1906).

42 Lawrence, *Magic of the Horse-Shoe*, p. 283.

43 Peter Kolb, *The Present State of the Cape of Good-Hope; or, A Particular Account of the Several Nations of the Hottentots . . .* , trans. Mr Medley (London, 1731), pp. 98–9.

44 Mariano Edward Rivero and John James von Tschudi, *Peruvian Antiquities*, trans. Francis L. Hawks (New York, 1853), p. 197.

45 Kenneth Patchen, 'A Message From the Assistant Chief of the Fly

People', in *The Collected Poems of Kenneth Patchen* (New York, 1968), p. 464.

46 *The Epic of Gilgamesh*, trans. Andrew George (London, 1999), p. 94.

47 Ibid.

3 STICKY FUN

1 Christopher Smart, *The Poetical Works of Christopher Smart*, vol. 1: *Jubilate Agno*, ed. Karina Williamson (Oxford, 1980), p. 10.

2 Vincent G. Dethier, *To Know A Fly* (San Francisco, 1962), pp. 23–4.

3 G. W. Barber and E. B. Starnes, 'The Activities of Houseflies', *Journal of the New York Entomological Society*, LVII (1949), pp. 203–14.

4 Thomas Blague, *A Schole of Wise Conceytes: Wherin as euery Conceyte hath wit, so the most haue much mirth, Set forth in common places by order of the Alphabet. Translated out of diuers Greke and Latine Wryters* (London, 1569), p. 138.

5 Francis Quarles, 'On A Flye', in *Divine Fancies: Digested into Epigrammes, Meditations and Observations* (London, 1632), p. 110.

6 John Quarles, 'God's Love and Man's Unworthiness', in *Divine Meditations upon Several Subjects* (London, 1655), p. 3.

7 George Keate, 'The Two Flies: A Fable', in *The Poetical Works of George Keate* (London, 1781), vol. 1, p. 148. References hereafter in the text.

8 George Wither, *A Collection of Emblemes, Ancient and Moderne, Quickened with metricall illustrations, both Morall and divine: And Disposed into lotteries, that instruction, and good counsell, may bee furthered by an honest and pleasant recreation* (London, 1635), p. 40.

9 Ben Jonson, 'The Hour-Glass', in *Ben Jonson: Poems*, ed. Ian Donaldson (London, New York and Toronto, 1975), p. 144.

10 Joseph Mitchell, 'On a Fly, Drown'd in a Lady's Eye', in *Poems on Several Occasions* (London, 1732), vol. 1, pp. 239–40.

11 Ibid., p. 240.

12 K. Langloh Piper, *Australian Legendary Tales: Folk-Lore of the Noongahburrahs as Told to the Piccaninnies*, 2nd edn (London and Melbourne, 1897), pp. 106–7.

13 Percy Bysshe Shelley, 'Queen Mab' (III. 106), in *The Complete Poetical Works of Percy Bysshe Shelley*, ed. Thomas Hutchinson, 2nd edn (London, New York and Toronto, 1970), p. 771.

14 Zofia Urbanowska, *Changé en mouche*, trans. and adapted Léon Golschmann and Ernest Jaubert (Paris, 1895), p. 31. References hereafter in the text and translations my own.

15 James. W. Redfield, *Comparative Physiognomy; or, Resemblances Between Men and Animals* (New York, 1852), p. 270. References hereafter in the text.

16 'Blowfly Beer for Online Beer', http://www.blowfly.com.au/ (accessed 10 July 2006).

17 Robert Dudley, 'Fermenting Fruit and the Historical Ecology of Ethanol Ingestion: Is Alcoholism in Modern Humans An Evolutionary Hangover?', *Addiction*, XCVII (2002), pp. 381–8.

18 Ulrike Heberlein et al., 'Molecular Genetic Analysis of Ethanol Intoxication in *Drosophila melanogaster*', *Integrative and Comparative Biology*, XLIV (2004), pp. 269–74.

19 Aristotle, *Historia animalium*, trans. D'Arcy Wentworth Thompson, *The Works of Aristotle*, ed. J. A. Smith and W. D. Ross, (Oxford, 1910), vol. IV, v. 8, 542a.

20 Lucian, 'The Fly', in *Lucian*, trans. by A. M. Harmon (London and New York, 1913), vol. I, p. 89.

21 Jim Heath, 'The Fly in Your Eye', http://www.viacorp.com/fly-book/fullgifs.html (accessed 10 July 2006).

22 Ralph Waldo Emerson, *English Traits: The Complete Works of Ralph Waldo Emerson* (Boston and New York, 1903–4), vol. V, p. 21.

23 Guy de Maupassant, 'Mouche', in *Contes et nouvelles*, ed. Louis Forestier (Paris, 1974), p. 1174.

24 Francine du Plessix Gray, *At Home with the Marquis de Sade* (London, 1999), pp. 127–31.

25 Edward Halford Ross, *The Reduction of Domestic Flies* (London, 1913), pp. 90–91.

26 *The Correspondence of Robert Boyle*, ed. Michael Hunter, Antonio Clericuzio and Lawrence Principe (London, 2001), vol. V, 1678–83, p. 468.

27 Martin Monestier, *Les Mouches: le pire ennemi de l'homme* (Paris, 2001), pp. 79 80.

28 Fleur Adcock, 'Coupling', in *Poems, 1960–2000* (Newcastle upon Tyne, 2000), p. 204.

29 Meleager, 'Against Mosquitoes' and 'The Mosquito', in *Poems From the Greek Anthology*, trans. Dudley Fitts (New York, 1956), pp. 25, 26.

30 James Joyce, *Ulysses: The Corrected Text*, ed. Hans Walter Gabler, Wolfhard Steppe and Claus Melchior (Harmondsworth, 1986), p. 144.

31 Roland Barthes, 'The Metaphor of the Eye', trans. J. A. Underwood, in Georges Bataille, *The Story of the Eye*, trans. Joachim Neugroschal (Harmondsworth, 1986), p. 121.

32 Ibid., p. 65.

4 ORDERS OF MAGNITUDE

1 William Kirby and William Spence, *An Introduction to Entomology; or, Elements of the Natural History of Insects* (London, 1815–26), vol. I, p. v.

2 Alexander Pope, *The Poems of Alexander Pope*, ed. John Butt (London and New Haven, 1951–), vol. v, *The Dunciad*, ed. James Sutherland, 3rd edn (1963), p. 385.

3 William Cowper, 'Charity', in *The Works of William Cowper*, ed. Robert Southey (London, 1835–7), vol. VIII, p. 244.

4 Ulisse Aldrovandi, *De Animalibus insectis libri septem* (Bologna, 1602): 'Ad lectorem' (unpaginated). My translation.

5 Henry Baker, *The Microscope Made Easy* (London, 1742), p. 221.

6 *Petronius*, with an English translation by Michael Heseltine (London and Cambridge, MA, 1961), p. 69.

7 Robert Hooke, *Micrographia; or, Some Physiological Descriptions of Minute Bodies Made by Magnifying Glasses* (London, 1665), p. 178.

8 Ibid., pp. 175–6.

9 Ibid., p. 180.

10 Leon Battista Alberti, 'Musca', in *Apologhi ed elogi*, ed. Rosario Contarino (Genoa, 1984), p. 184.

11 Pliny the Elder, *Natural History* (xxviii. 5), with an English translation by H. Rackham et al. (London, 1938–63), vol. viii, p. 23.

12 F. C. Lesser, *Théologie de insectes, ou démonstration des perfections de Dieu dans tout qui concerne les insectes* (trans. from German) (The Hague, 1742), vol. ii, pp. 188–9.

13 Aristotle, *Historia animalium*, trans. D'Arcy Wentworth Thompson, in *The Works of Aristotle*, ed. J. A. Smith and W. D. Ross (Oxford, 1910) vol. iv, v. 20, 553a.

14 Pliny, *Natural History* (xi. 43), vol. iii, p. 507.

15 Richard Brathwaite, *A Strange Metamorphosis of Man, Transformed Into a Wildernesse Deciphered in Characters* (London, 1634), sig F1r.

16 D'Arcy Wentworth Thompson, 'Greek Children's Games', Letter to the Editor, *Discovery*, iv (1923), p. 56.

17 Fred W. Saxby, 'How to Photograph Through a Fly's Eye', *Knowledge: An Illustrated Magazine of Science*, n.s. 13, xxi (1898), p. 189.

18 Ted Hughes, 'Fly Inspects', in *Collected Poems* (London, 2003), p. 632.

19 Ibid., pp. 632–3.

20 Baker, *Microscope Made Easy*, p. 298.

21 Gilles Deleuze and Félix Guattari, *A Thousand Plateaus: Capitalism and Schizophrenia*, trans. Brian Massumi (London, 1988), p. 239.

22 Kirby and Spence, *Introduction to Entomology*, vol. ii, p. 362.

23 Hooke, *Micrographia*, p. 173.

24 Robert W. Matthews and Janice R. Matthews, *Insect Behavior* (New York, 1978), pp. 77–8.

25 F. W. Fitzsimons, *The House Fly: A Slayer of Men* (London, 1915), pp. 9–10.

26 Antony de Bartolo, 'Buzz Off!', *Chicago Tribune* (5 June 1986), http://www.hydeparkmedia.com/housefly.html (accessed 1 February 2005); Hannah Holmes, 'Where Fruit Flies Come From', http://www.discovery.com/area/skinnyon/skinnyon970718/skinny1.html (accessed 4 August 2005).

27 Leo H. Grindon, *Life: Its Nature, Varieties and Phenomena* (Philadelphia, 1867), p. 122n.

28 Anonymous review of P. H. Gosse, *Life in Its Lower, Intermediate and Higher Forms; or, Manifestations of the Divine Wisdom in the*

Natural History of Animals (New York, 1857), in *Princeton Review*,
XXIX (1857), p. 330

29 Baker, *Microscope Made Easy*, pp. 303, 305–6.

30 Mark Twain, *Letters From the Earth*, ed. Bernard Devoto (New York,
Evanston, IL, and London, 1962), pp. 24–5. References in the text
hereafter.

5 FLY WARS

1 Kethuboth 77b; Isaac Harpaz, 'Early Entomology in the Middle
East', in *History of Entomology*, ed. Ray Smith, Thomas E. Mittler
and Carroll N. Smith (Palo Alto, CA, 1973), p. 33.

2 Pliny the Elder, *Natural History* (x. 40), with an English translation by H. Rackham et al. (London, 1938–63), vol. III, p. 341.

3 *The Works of Thomas Sydenham*, trans. R. G. Latham (London,
1848), vol. I, p. 271.

4 Muhammad ibn Musa Ad-Damiri, *Ad-Damitri's Hayat al-Hayawan
(A Zoological Lexicon)*, trans. A.S.G. Jayakar (London and Bombay,
1906–8), vol. I, p. 822.

5 Jan Knappert, *The Enyclopaedia of Middle Eastern Mythology and
Religion* (Shaftesbury, 1993), p. 125.

6 Pliny, *Natural History* (XXIX. 34), vol. VIII, p. 251; F. C. Lesser,
*Théologie des insectes, ou démonstration des perfections de Dieu dans
tout qui concerne les insectes* (trans. from German) (The Hague,
1742), vol. II, p. 188.

7 Pliny, *Natural History* (XXX. 34, XXX. 41), vol. VIII, pp. 347, 357.

8 Vincent J. Cirillo 'Fever and Reform: The Typhoid Epidemic in the
Spanish-American War', *Journal of the History of Medicine and
Allied Sciences*, LV (2000), pp. 363–97.

9 Walter Reed, Victor C. Vaughan and Edward O. Shakespeare,
*Abstract of Report on the Origin and Spread of Typhoid Fever in US
Military Camps during the Spanish War of 1898* (Washington, DC,
1900), p. 231.

10 Samuel Beckett, 'Serena I', in *Collected Poems in English and French*
(London, 1977), p. 22.

11 J. Niven, 'Summer Diarrhoea and Enteric Fever', *Proceedings of the Royal Society of Medicine*, III (1910), pp. 131–216.

12 Naomi Rogers, 'Germs with Legs: Flies, Disease and the New Public Health', *Bulletin of the History of Medicine*, LXIII (1989), pp. 599–617.

13 'Flies', in *All The Year Round*, VIII (1862–3), p. 7.

14 F. Fitzsimons, *The House Fly: A Slayer of Men* (London, 1915), p. v. References in text hereafter.

15 Edward Halford Ross, *The Reduction of Domestic Flies* (London, 1913), p. 8. References in text hereafter.

16 Naomi Rogers, 'Dirt, Flies and Immigrants: Explaining the Epidemiology of Poliomyelitis', *Journal of the History of Medicine and Allied Sciences*, XLIV (1989), p. 498.

17 Thomas Say, 'Some Account of the Insect Known by the Name of Hessian Fly, and of a Parasitic Insect That Feeds Upon It', *Journal of the Academy of Natural Sciences*, III (1817), pp. 9–54, 73–104

18 George Morgan to John Temple, 26 August 1788, copy in Thomas Jefferson Papers, Manuscripts Division, Library of Congress, Washington, DC, quoted by Philip J. Pauly, in 'Fighting the Hessian Fly: American and British Responses to Insect Invasion, 1776–1789', *Environmental History*, VII (2002), p. 485.

19 Henry Ward Beecher, *Eyes and Ears* (Boston, MA, 1862), p. 69

20 Eleanor A. Ormerod, *The Hessian Fly in Great Britain in 1887: Being Mainly Reports of British Observations with Illustrations and Some Means of Remedy* (London, 1887).

21 Grant Allen, 'A Foreign Invasion of England', *Strand Magazine*, XVI (July 1898), p. 97.

22 R. W. Hope, 'On Insects and their Larvae Occasionally Found in the Human Body', *Transactions of the Royal Entomological Society of London*, II (1840), p. 258.

23 W. S. Patton, 'Notes on the Myiasis-Producing Diptera of Man and Animals', *Bulletin of Entomological Research*, XII (1921), pp. 239–61.

24 Adrian Forsyth, 'Jerry's Botfly', in *Insect Lives: Stories of Mystery and Romance from a Hidden World*, ed. Erich Hoyt and Ted Schultz (Cambridge, MA, 1999), pp. 253–8.

25 Maurice T. James, *The Flies That Cause Myiasis in Man*
    (Washington, DC, 1947), pp. 03–5.

26 Lactantius, *A Relation of the Death of the Primitive Persecutors*,
    trans. Gilbert Burnet (Amsterdam, 1687), pp. 129–30.

27 Jan Bondeson, *A Cabinet of Medical Curiosities* (London and New
    York, 1997), p. 67.

28 D.-J. Larrey, *Clinique chirurgicale, exercé particulièrement dans les
    camps et les hopitaux [sic] militaires, depuis 1792 jusqu'en 1829*
    (Paris and Montpellier, 1829), vol. I, pp. 51–2.

29 Robert and Michèle Root-Bernstein, *Honey, Mud, Maggots and
    Other Medical Marvels* (London, 1999), pp. 22–3.

30 *Medical Insects and Arachnids*, ed. Richard P. Lane and Roger W.
    Crosskey (London, 1993), p. 459.

31 Martin Monestier, *Les Mouches: le pire ennemi de l'homme* (Paris,
    2004).

6 MUTABLE FLY

1 Wolfram Eberhard, *Chinese Fairy Tales and Folk Tales* (London,
   1937), pp. 254–5.

2 Hermann Usener, *Götternamen: Versuch einer Lehre von der
   religiösen Begriffsbildung* (Bonn, 1896), pp. 279–301.

3 Aristotle, *Historia animalium*, trans. D'Arcy Wentworth
   Thompson, in *The Works of Aristotle*, ed. J. A. Smith and W. D.
   Ross (Oxford, 1910), vol. IV, v. 1, 539a–539b.

4 Ibid., v. 19, 552b.

5 Pliny the Elder, *Natural History* (XI. 42), with an English translation by H. Rackham et al. (London, 1938–63), vol. III, p. 507.

6 Lucian, 'The Fly', in *Lucian*, trans. A. M. Harmon (London and
   New York, 1913), vol. I, p. 85.

7 Ibid.

8 St John Chrysostom, *Homilies on the Acts of the Apostles* (Homily
   VII. 4), Patrologia Graeca, ed. J. P. Migne (Paris, 1857–66), vol. LX,
   cols 69–70.

9 Augustine of Hippo, *Against Faustus the Manichean* (XIX. 22),

Patrologia Latina, ed. J. P. Migne (Paris, 1845–65), vol. XLII, col. 361. My translation.

10 *The Catholic Encyclopedia*, ed. Charles G. Herbermann et al. (New York, 1907–12), vol. IV, p.784.

11 St John Chrysostom, *Homilies on the Gospel of St John* (Homily II. 2, John 1. 1), Patrologia Graeca, vol. LIX, col. 31. My translation.

12 St John Chrysostom, *Homilies on the Acts of the Apostles* (Homily IV. 4, Acts 2. 1, 2), Patrologia Graeca, vol. LX, pp. 47–8. My translation.

13 *The Seven Books of Arnobius Adversus Gentes* (II. 47), trans. Archibald Hamilton Bryce and Hugh Campbell, in *Ante-Nicene Christian Library: Translations of the Writings of the Fathers Down to AD 325*, ed. Alexander Roberts and James Donaldson, vol. XIX (Edinburgh, 1871), pp. 114–15.

14 Ogden Nash, 'The Fly', in *Collected Verse from 1929 on* (London, 1961), p. 333.

15 *Mark Twain's Fables of Man*, ed. John S. Tuckey (Berkeley, Los Angeles and London, 1972), p. 112

16 Augustine of Hippo, *On The Gospel of St John* (Tractate I. 14), *Patrologia Latina*, ed. J. P. Migne, vol. XXXV, col. 1386. My translation.

17 Augustine of Hippo, *Of Two Souls: Against the Manicheans*, Patrologia Latina, ed. J. P. Migne, vol. XLII, col. 96. My translation.

18 Muhammad ibn Musa Ad-Dimiri, *Ad-Damiri's Hayat al-Hayawan (A Zoological Lexicon)*, trans. A.S.G. Jayakar (London and Bombay, 1906–8), vol. I, p. 823.

19 Edward Topsell, *The History of Four-footed Beasts and Serpents . . . Whereunto is now added, The Theater of Insects; or, Lesser Living Creatures: As Bees, Flies, Caterpillars, Spiders, Worms, &c. A most elaborate work: by T. Muffet, Dr of Physick* (London, 1658), pp. 944, 946.

20 Francesco Redi, *Esperienze intorno alla generazione degl'insetti* (Florence, 1688).

21 John Swammerdam, *Ephemeri Vita; or, The Natural History and Anatomy of the Ephemeron, a Fly That Lives But Five Hours*, trans. Edward Tyson (London, 1681), pp. 1–2

22 Richard Bentley, *A Confutation of Atheism From the Structure and*

Origin of Humane Bodies. Part II: A Sermon Preached at St Mary-le-Bow June 6. 1692 (London, 1692), p. 22.

23 Ibid., p. 29.

24 Ibid.

25 Noël Antoine Pluche, *Spectacle de la nature; or, Nature Display'd* (London, 1770), vol. I/1, p. 34.

26 F. C. Lesser, *Théologie des insectes; ou, démonstration des perfections de Dieu dans tout qui concerne les insects*, trans. from German (The Hague, 1742), vol. I, pp. 84–5.

27 William Wordsworth, *The Excursion*, Book 1, l. 596, in *The Poetical Works of William Wordsworth*, ed. Ernest de Selincourt and Helen Darbishire (Oxford, 1940–9), vol. V, p. 28.

28 Ibid., p. 122.

29 Johann Wolfgang von Goethe, *The Sorrows of Young Werther*, trans. Michael Hulse (Harmondsworth, 1989), pp. 26–7.

30 Edward Poulson, *The Wonders of the Microscope and Design in Creation, With Remarks Upon Disease Spread By Flies* (London, 1896), p. 16.

31 Pierre Ramus, *Scholarum mathematicarum libri unus et triginta* (Basle, 1569), p. 65. My translation.

32 Guillaume de Salluste du Bartas, 'The Sixt Day of the First Weeke', in *Du Bartas: His Divine Weekes and Workes*, trans. Josuah Sylvester (London, 1621), p. 134.

33 One of the most influential retellings of the story is in the book of diversions that Gervase of Tilbury wrote for the Emperor Otto IV, *Otia Imperialia: Recreation for an Emperor*, ed. and trans. S. E. Banks and J. W. Binns (Oxford, 2002), pp. 576–7, although the first written version of the story was recorded by John of Salisbury in his *Policraticus* of about 1159. J. Pip Wilson, 'Virgil: The Poet as Magician' http://www.wilsonsalmanac.com/virgil.html (accessed 13 July 2006).

34 Silvio A. Bedini, 'The Role of Automata in the History of Technology', *Technology and Culture*, IV (1964), p. 32, http://xroads.virginia.edu/~DRBR/b_edini.html (accessed 13 July 2006).

35 M. P. Verneuil, in *The Craftsman*, v/6 (1904), pp. 567–8, quoted in Suzanne Tennenbaum and Janet Zapata, *The Jeweled Menagerie: The World of Animals in Gems* (London, 2001), p. 13.

36 Robert Herrick, 'The Amber Bead', in *Poetical Works*, ed. F. W. Moorman (Oxford, 1915), p. 269.

37 William Hayley, 'Essay on Painting', in *Poems and Plays* (London, 1788), vol. I, p. 40.

38 'The Fair Moralist', in *The Works of the Right Honourable Sir Chas. Hanbury Williams* (London, 1822), vol. III, pp. 111–12.

39 Aelian, *On The Characteristics of Animals* (xv. i), with an English translation by A. F. Scholfield (London and Cambridge, MA, 1958–9), vol. III, pp. 203–4.

40 John Dennys, *The Secrets of Angling* (London, 1620), sig. c5r.

41 Thomas Barker, *Barker's Delight; or, The Art of Angling* (London, 1656), pp. 7–13.

42 Charles Cotton, *The Compleat Angler: Being Instructions How to Angle for Trout or Grayling in a Clear Stream: Part II* (London, 1676), pp. 68–82.

43 Alfred Ronalds, *The Fly-Fisher's Entomology*, new edn (London, 1921), p. xxvii.

44 May R. Berenbaum, *Bugs in The System: Insects and Their Impact on Human Affairs* (Reading, MA, 1995), p. 266.

45 J. C. Mottram, *Fly Fishing: Some New Arts and Mysteries* (London, 1915).

46 John Waller Hills, *A History of Fly Fishing for Trout* (London, 1921), p. 74.

47 Mottram, *Fly-Fishing*, pp. 62–3.

48 Mikael Frödin, *Classic Salmon Flies: History and Patterns* (Moffat, 1991); Paul Schmookler and Ingrid V. Sils, *Rare and Unusual Fly Tying Materials: A Natural History. Volume 1 – Birds.* (Millis, MA, 1994); W. B. Yeats, 'The Fisherman' and 'Sailing to Byzantium', in *The Poems*, ed. Richard J. Finneran (Basingstoke and London, 1993), pp. 148, 194.

49 Norbert Boedekker and Martin Engelhaaf, 'Steering a Virtual Blowfly: Simulation of Visual Pursuit', *Proceedings of the Royal*

Society of London B, CCLXX (2003), pp. 1971–8.

50 Michael H. Dickinson, 'Come Fly With Me', *Engineering and Science*, III (2003), pp. 10–19.

51 Philip Pullman, *Northern Lights* (London, 1995), pp. 134–7.

52 François Jacob, 'The Fly', in *Of Flies, Mice and Men*, trans. Giselle Weiss (Cambridge, MA, and London, 1998), p. 34.

53 Martin Brookes, *Fly: The Unsung Hero of Twentieth-Century Science* (London, 2001), pp. 38–40.

54 George Langelaan, 'The Fly', in *Out of Time* (London, 1964), pp. 7–41.

55 Jacob, 'The Fly', p. 39.

56 Ibid., p. 46.

57 Vincent G. Dethier, *The Hungry Fly: A Physiological Study of the Behavior Associated with Feeding* (Cambridge, MA, and London, 1976), p. 1.

58 M. D. Adams et al., 'The Genome Sequence of *Drosophila melanogaster*', *Science*, CCLXXXVII (2000), pp. 2185–95.

59 Vincent G. Dethier, *To Know A Fly* (San Francisco, 1962), p. 77.

60 Balaji Krishnan, Stuart E. Dryer and Paul E. Hardin, 'Circadian Rhythms in Olfactory Responses of *Drosophila melanogaster*', *Nature*, 400.6742 (1999), pp. 375–8.

61 Aristotle, *Historia animalium*, V. 19, 552b.

62 Aelian, *On The Characteristics of Animals* (II. 4), vol. I, p. 91.

63 Michael R. Rose and Margarida Matos, 'The Creation of Methuselah Flies By Laboratory Evolution', in *Methuselah Flies: A Case Study in the Evolution of Aging*, ed. Michael R. Rose, Hardip B. Passananti and Margarida Matos (Singapore, 2004), pp. 3–9.

64 Yi-Jyun Lin, Laurent Seroude, and Seymour Benzer, 'Extended Life-Span and Stress Resistance in the *Drosophila* Mutant *Methuselah*', *Science*, CCLXXXVII (1998), pp. 943–6.

65 Anthony Timpone, 'David Cronenberg: Lord of the Fly', http://www.davidcronenberg.de/fangofly1.html (accessed 13 July 2006).

66 *Cronenberg on Cronenberg*, ed. Chris Rodley (London and Boston, MA, 1992), p. 125.

67 Ibid., p. 80.

68 Michael Crichton, *Jurassic Park* (New York, 1990).

69 George and Roberta Poinar, *The Quest for Life in Amber* (Reading, MA, 1994).

70 George Poinar, 'Insects in Amber', *Annual Review of Entomology*, XXXVIII (1993), pp. 145–59.

7 FLY LEAVES

1 Virgil, *Georgics* (3. 146–56), in *Virgil*, with an English translation by H. Rushton Fairclough, rev. G. P. Goold (Cambridge, MA, and London, 1999), vol. I, p. 187.

2 *Reallexikon für Antike und Christentum: Sachwörterbuch zur Auseinandersetzung des Christentums mit der antiken Welt*, ed. Theodor Klauser (Stuttgart, 1950–), vol. VII, cols 1114–15.

3 Muhammad ibn 'Abd Allah Kisa'i, *The Tales of the Prophets of al-Kisa'i*, trans. W. M. Thackston, Jr (Boston, MA, 1978), p. 150.

4 Percy Bysshe Shelley, 'The Witch of Atlas', *The Complete Poetical Works of Percy Bysshe Shelley*, ed. Thomas Hutchinson, 2nd edn (London, New York and Toronto, 1970), l. 364, p. 380; John Keats, *Endymion* (I. 852–4), in *Poetical Works*, ed. H. W. Garrod (London, Oxford and New York, 1970), p. 76.

5 Robert Lloyd, *Poetical Works* (London, 1762), vol. I, p.51.

6 Miguel de Cervantes, *The Life and Notable Adventures of That Renown'd Knight, Don Quixote De la Mancha, Merrily Translated Into Hudibrastick Verse*, trans. Edward Ward (London, 1711–12), vol. I, p. 188.

7 William Cowper, 'The Progress of Error', in *The Works of William Cowper*, ed. Robert Southey (London, 1835–7), vol. VIII, p. 155.

8 Samuel Wesley, *Maggots; or, Poems on Several Subjects, Never Before Handled* (London, 1685), p. 1.

9 E. N. Lorenz, *The Essence of Chaos* (Seattle, WA, 1993), pp. 181–4.

10 Ray Bradbury, 'A Sound of Thunder', in *R is for Rocket* (London, 1968), pp. 79–93.

11 Ian C. Beavis, *Insects and Other Invertebrates in Classical Antiquity*

(Exeter, 1998), p. 231.

12 Aristotle, *Historia animalium*, trans. D'Arcy Wentworth Thompson, in *The Works of Aristotle*, ed. J. A. Smith and W. D. Ross, (Oxford, 1910), vol. IV, v. 1, 539a–535b.

13 Aristophanes, *The Clouds*, in *Aristophanes*, ed. and trans. Jeffrey Henderson (Cambridge, MA, and London, 1998–2002), vol. II, pp. 28–9.

14 Thomas Browne, *Pseudodoxia Epidemica; or, Enquiries into Very Many Received Tenents and Commonly Presumed Truths*, in *The Works of Thomas Browne*, ed. Geoffrey Keynes (London, 1964), vol. II, p. 260.

15 William Kirby and William Spence, *An Introduction to Entomology; or, Elements of the Natural History of Insects* (London, 1815–26), vol. II, p.375.

16 Thomas Inman, *Ancient Faiths Embodied in Ancient Names* (London and Liverpool, 1868–9), vol. I, pp. 328–9.

17 Lucian, 'The Fly', in *Lucian*, trans. A. M. Harmon (London and New York, 1913), vol. I, pp. 91–3.

18 P. Amaury Talbot, *In The Shadow of the Bush* (London, 1912), pp. 384–5.

19 Francis Quarles, 'Job Militant', in *Divine Poems* (London, 1632), p. 229.

20 James Wright, *Country Conversations* (London, 1694), p. 2.

21 Edward Young, *Night Thoughts on Life, Death and Immortality: In Nine Nights. Complete Works* (London, 1854), vol. I, p. 99.

22 FOLDOC: *Free On-Line Dictionary of Computing*, http://wombat.doc.ic.ac.uk/foldoc/foldoc.cgi?query=buzz&action=Search (accessed 25 April 2005).

23 Leon Battista Alberti, 'Musca', in *Apologhi ed elogi*, ed. Rosario Contarino (Genoa, 1984), pp. 187–9.

24 Archibald Alison, 'Of the Sublimity and Beauty of Sound', in *Essays on the Nature and Principles of Taste* (Edinburgh, 1790), pp. 144–5.

25 Keats, *Poetical Works*, p. 259.

26 Ibid., p. 274.

27 Marcel Proust, *Remembrance of Things Past*, trans. C. K. Scott-

Moncrieff and Terence Kilmartin (London, 1981), vol. I, p. 89.

28 Emily Dickinson, *Complete Poems*, ed. Thomas H. Johnson (London, 1970), pp. 223–4.

29 Ambrose Bierce, *The Unabridged Devil's Dictionary*, ed. David E. Schultz (Athens, GA, and London, 2000), p. 83.

30 Ibid.

31 Eric Partridge, *The Routledge Dictionary of Historical Slang* (London, 1973), p. 334.

32 Bierce, *Devil's Dictionary*, pp. 83–4.

33 Ibid., p. 230.

34 Martin Heidegger, *The Fundamental Concepts of Metaphysics: World, Finitude, Solitude*, trans. William McNeill and Nicolas Walker (Bloomington, IN, 1995), p. 177.

35 Francis Quarles, 'A Feast for Wormes', in *Divine Poems* (London, 1623), p. 5.

36 Robert E. Kohler, *Lords of the Fly:* Drosophila *Genetics and the Experimental Life* (Chicago and London, 1994), p. 19.

37 Charles Bukowksi, '2 Flies', in *Play the Piano Drunk Like a Percussion Instrument until The Fingers Begin To Bleed a Bit* (Santa Rosa, CA, 1979), p. 35.

38 Michel Serres and Bruno Latour, *Conversations on Science, Culture and Time*, trans. Roxanne Lapidus (Ann Arbor, MI, 1995), p. 6.

Bibliography

Adams, M. D., et al., 'The Genome Sequence of *Drosophila melanogaster*', *Science*, 287 (2000), pp. 2185–95

Ad-Damiri, Muhammad ibn Musa, *Ad-Damiri's Hayāt al-Hayawān (A Zoological Lexicon)*, trans. A.S.G. Jayakar, 2 vols (London and Bombay, 1906–8)

Alberti, Leon Battista, 'Musca', in *Apologhi ed elogi*, ed. Rosario Contarino (Genoa, 1984), pp. 173–85

Aldrovandi, Ulisse, *De animalibus insectis libri septem* (Bologna, 1602)

Aristotle, *Historia animalium*, trans. D'Arcy Wentworth Thompson (Oxford, 1910)

Bay, André, *Des mouches et des hommes* (Paris, 1979)

Beavis, Ian C., *Insects and Other Invertebrates in Classical Antiquity* (Exeter, 1998)

Brookes, Martin, *Fly: The Unsung Hero of Twentieth-century Science* (London, 2001)

Crémieux, Hector, and Ludovic Halévy, *Orpheus in the Underworld: Operetta in Three Acts*, trans. Geoffrey Dunn (London, 1981)

Dethier, Vincent G., *To Know a Fly* (San Francisco, 1962)

—, *The Hungry Fly: A Physiological Study of the Behavior Associated with Feeding* (Cambridge, MA, and London, 1976)

Dudley, Robert, 'Fermenting Fruit and the Historical Ecology of Ethanol Ingestion: Is Alcoholism in Modern Humans an Evolutionary Hangover?', *Addiction*, XCVII (2002), pp. 381–8

Fitzsimons, F. W., *The House Fly: A Slayer of Men* (London, 1915)

Glanvill, Joseph, *Saducismus Triumphatus; or, Full and Plain Evidence*

Concerning Witches and Apparitions. In Two Parts. The First Treating of their Possibility; The Second of their Real Existence, 3rd edn (London, 1681)

The Epic of Gilgamesh, trans. Andrew George (London, 1999)

Golding, William, *Lord of the Flies* (London, 1996)

Harpaz, Isaac, 'Early Entomology in the Middle East', in *History of Entomology*, ed. Ray Smith, Thomas E. Mittler and Carroll N. Smith (Palo Alto, CA, 1973), pp. 21–36

Homer, *Iliad*, trans. A. T. Murray, rev. William F. Wyatt, 2 vols (Cambridge, MA, and London, 1999)

Hooke, Robert, *Micrographia; or, Some Physiological Descriptions of Minute Bodies Made by Magnifying Glasses* (London, 1665)

Hughes, Ted, 'Fly Inspects', in *Collected Poems* (London, 2003), p. 632

Jacob, François, 'The Fly', in *Of Flies, Mice and Men*, trans. Giselle Weiss (Cambridge, MA, and London, 1998), pp. 27–46

James, Maurice T., *The Flies That Cause Myiasis in Man* (Washington, DC, 1947)

Keate, George, 'The Two Flies: A Fable', in *The Poetical Works of George Keate*, 2 vols (London, 1781), vol. I, p. 148

Kirby, William, and William Spence, *An Introduction to Entomology; or, Elements of the Natural History of Insects*, 4 vols (London, 1815–26)

Kohler, Robert E., *Lords of the Fly:* Drosophila *Genetics and the Experimental Life* (Chicago and London, 1994)

Kritsky, Gene, 'Tombs, Mummies, and Flies', *Bulletin of the Entomological Association of America*, XXXI (1985), pp. 18–19

Langelaan, George, 'The Fly', in *Out of Time* (London, 1964), pp. 7–41

Lesser, F. C., *Théologie de insects; ou, démonstration des perfections de Dieu dans tout qui concerne les insectes* (The Hague, 1742) [trans. from German]

Lucian, 'The Fly', in *Lucian*, trans. A. M. Harmon, 8 vols (London, 1913), vol. I, pp. 82–95

Maclaurin, E.C.B., 'Beelzeboul', in *Novum Testamentum*, XX (1978), pp. 156–60

Mitchell, Joseph, 'On a Fly, Drown'd in a Lady's Eye', in *Poems on Several Occasions*, 2 vols (London, 1732), vol. I, pp. 238–40

Moffett, Thomas, *The Theater of Insects; or, Lesser Living Creatures: As Bees, Flies, Caterpillars, Spiders, Worms, &c.* (London, 1658)

Monestier, Martin, *Les Mouches: le pire ennemi de l'homme* (Paris, 2004)

Ormerod, Eleanor A., *The Hessian Fly in Great Britain in 1887: Being Mainly Reports of British Observations with Illustrations and Some Means of Remedy* (London, 1887)

Pliny the Elder, *Natural History*, trans. H. Rackham et al., 10 vols (London, 1938–63)

Quarles, Francis, 'On a Flye', in *Divine Fancies: Digested into Epigrammes, Meditations and Observations* (London, 1632), p. 10

—, 'God's Love and Man's Unworthiness', in *Divine Meditations upon Several Subjects* (London, 1655), p. 3

Redi, Francesco, *Esperienze intorno alla generazione degl'insetti* (Florence, 1688)

Rogers, Naomi, 'Germs with Legs: Flies, Disease and the New Public Health', *Bulletin of the History of Medicine*, LXIII (1989), pp. 599–617

—, 'Dirt, Flies and Immigrants: Explaining the Epidemiology of Poliomyelitis', *Journal of the History of Medicine and Allied Sciences*, XLIV (1989), pp. 486–505

Root-Bernstein, Robert, and Michèle Root-Bernstein, *Honey, Mud, Maggots and Other Medical Marvels* (London, 1999)

Ross, Edward Halford, *The Reduction of Domestic Flies* (London, 1913)

Swammerdam, John, *Ephemeri Vita; or, The Natural History and Anatomy of the Ephemeron, a Fly That Lives But Five Hours*, trans. Edward Tyson (London, 1681)

Urbanowska, Zofia, *Changé en mouche*, trans. Léon Golschmann and Ernest Jaubert (Paris, 1895)

The Zend-Avesta. Part I: The Vendîdâd, trans. James Darmesteter (Delhi, 1995)

Associations and Websites

ARBRITSKREIS DIPTERA
www.ak-diptera.de
German diptera site.

ONLINE CATALOGUE OF THE
FOSSIL FLIES OF THE WORLD
http://hbs.bishopmuseum.org/
fossilcat/
By Neal L. Evenhuis.

DIPTERA.INFO
http://www.diptera.info/news.
php
Dutch diptera site maintained
by Paul Beuk.

DIPTERA LINKS
http://www.ent.iastate.edu/list/
directory/85/vid/5>
A page maintained by the Iowa
State Entomology Index of
Internet Resources.

THE DIPTERA SITE
www.sel.barc.usda.gov/Diptera/
Maintained by the Smithsonian
and Systematic Entomology
Laboratory, Washington, DC

DIPTERISTS' CLUB OF JAPAN
http://furumusi.aez.jp/dipter-
ist/dipterist.htm

DIPTERISTS FORUM
www.dipteristsforum.org.uk
A society devoted to the study of
diptera in Britain. Contact
address: Dipterists Forum, c/o
BENHS, The Pelham-Clinton
Building, Dinton Pastures
Country Park, Hurst, Reading,
RG10 OTH.

FLYBASE
http://flybase.bio.indiana.edu/
A database of the Drosophila
genome.

FLYBRAIN
http://flybrain.neurobio.
arizona.edu/
An atlas and database of the
Drosophila nervous system.

FLYMOVE
http://flymove.uni-
muenster.de/Homepage.html

FLY TIMES
www.nadsdiptera.org/New/FlyT
imes/Flyhome.htm
Newsletter of the North
American Diptera Society.

HOVERFLIES DISCUSSION GROUP
http://groups.yahoo.com/group
/UK-Hoverflies

THE INTERACTIVE FLY
http://flybase.bio.indiana.edu/a
llied-data/lk/Interactive-
fly/aimain/1aahome.htm
A Guide to Drosophila
Development.

THE MALLOCH SOCIETY
http://www.mallochsociety.org.
uk/
A Scottish site, named after the
eminent Scottish dipterist John
Russell Malloch (1875–1963).

Photo Acknowledgements

The author and publishers wish to express their thanks to the below sources of illustrative material and/or permission to reproduce it. (Some locations uncredited in the captions for reasons of brevity are also given below.)

Ashmolean Museum, Oxford: p. 138 (foot); photo Stan Baird (by permission of Arco-Iris): p. 100; British Library, London (photos British Library Reproductions): pp. 35 (*Isabella Breviary*, Add. MS 18851, f. 309), 44 (*Isabella Breviary*, f. 71), 97 (*Gorleston Psalter*, Add 49622 f. 7v), 142 (C107 e 91); photos British Library Reproductions: pp. 8, 50 (from Peter Kolb, *The Present State of the Cape of Good-Hope: or a Particular Account of the Several Nations of the Hottentots with a short account of the Dutch settlement at the Cape*, London, 1731), 65 (from James Samuelson and J. Braxton-Hicks, *Humble Creatures: The Earthworm and the Housefly . . .*, London, 1858), 79 (from Henry Louis Stephens, *The Death and Burial of Poor Cock Robin*, New York and London, 1864), 91 (from Johan Rudolf Schellenberg, *Genres des mouches Diptères représentés en XLII planches projettées et dessinées et expliquées par deux amatuers de l'entomologie/ Gattungen der Fliegen in XLII. Kupfertafeln entworfen und gezeichnet von J. R. Schellenberg, und erklärt durch zwey Leibhaber der Intsektenkunde*, Zürich, 1803), 103, 126 (both from Wilhelm Friedrich von Gleichen-Russworm, *Geschichte der gemeinen Stubenfliege*, Nuremberg, 1790), 134 (from *Esperiensi intorno alla generazione degl'insette fatte da Francesco Redi . . .*, Florence, 1688); British Museum, London: pp. 20, 175; photo Tove Dahlström: p. 141; from John Dennys, *The secrets of angling. Teaching, the choisest tooles, baytes and seasons, for the taking of any fish, in pond or river: practised and familiarly opened in three bookes* (London, 1635): p. 145

(top): from F. W. Fitzsimons, *The House Fly: A Slayer of Men* (London, 1915): pp. 14, 109; Galleria Nazionale di Capodimonte, Naples: pp. 180, 181; Galleria Nazionale di Palazzo Corsini, Rome: p. 28; from Johannes Goedaert, *De insectis in methodum redactus, cum notularum additione . . .* (London, 1685): p. 127; photo Philip Gross: p. 55; from Robert Hooke, *Micrographia, Or, Some Physiological Descriptions of Minute Bodies Made by Magnifying Glasses* (London, 1665): pp. 83, 86 (left), 120, 138 (top); photos Nigel Jones: p. 34, 161; Koninklijk Museum voor Schone Kunsten, Antwerp: p. 15; photos Library of Congress, Washington, DC: p. 106 top right (Prints and Photographs Division, Work Projects Administration Poster Collection, LC-USZC2-1952), 110 (Prints and Photographs Division, Work Projects Administration Poster Collection, LC-USZC2-5437), 111 (Prints Printed Ephemera Collection, Portfolio 64, Folder 33), 131 (Prints and Photographs Division, LC-USZ62-84276), 167 foot (from Jehosophat Aspin, *A familiar treatise on astronomy . . .*, 1825, LC-USZC4-10064); photo Mark Merton: p. 158; from Thomas Moffett, *The Theater of Insects; or, Lesser Living Creatures: As Bees, Flies, Caterpillars, Spiders, Worms, &c . . .* (London, 1658): pp. 86 (right), 167 (top), 179; Musée du Louvre, Paris: p. 67; Museum für Kunst und Kulturgeschichte, Dortmund: p. 27; photos National Library of Medicine, Bethesda, Maryland: pp. 18, 21, 57, 102, 104, 112, 122; from Gabriel Naudaeus, *The History of Magick By way of Apology, For all the Wise Men who have unjustly been reputed Magicians, from the Creation, to the present Age* (London, 1657): p. 39 (lower right); photos New York Public Library: pp. 58, 107, 115; Palazzo Pitti, Florence (Galleria Palatina): p. 60; from Claude Paradin, *The heroicall devises of M. Claudius Paradin*, London, 1591): p. 67; from John Payne, *Animalium quadrupedum avium florum* (London, 1625): pp. 45, 81; from Guillaume de la Perriere, *The theater of fine deuices containing an hundred morall emblemes* (London, 1614): p. 98; from Collin de Plancy, *Dictionnaire infernale* (Paris, 1863): p. 39 (lower left); photos Rex Features: pp. 10 (Rex Features/Chris Martin Bahr, 254101Q), 48 (Rex Features/Roger Viollet, RV-312801), 71 (Rex Features/Kimmo Taskinen, 537864I), 96 (Rex Features/Roger-Viollet, 454239CD), 106 (top left) (Rex Features/Roger-Viollet, HRL-636392A), 113 (Rex Features/Roger Viollet, BOY-15813); from Paul Schmookler and Ingrid Sils, *Rare and Unusual Fly Tying Materials: A*

Natural History Treating Both Standard and Rare Materials, Their Sources and Geography, as Used in Classic, Contemporary, and Artistic Trout and Salmon Flies . . ., vol. 1: *Birds* (Mills, Massachusetts, 1997): p. 148; photos Nigel Smith: pp. 73, 144; Szëpmüvészeti Müzeum, Budapest: p. 74; from *The Fables of Aesop and Others* (London, 1857): p. 80; photo Steve Thomas: p. 121; © Andrew Toos/www.CartoonStock.com: p. 154; photos Brian Valentine: pp. 6, 11, 23, 56 (foot), 82, 85; photos John Vallender pp. 16, 22, 145 (foot), 151, 185; Virtual Fossil Museum <www.fossilmuseum.net>: pp. 143, 164 (left, right), 165 (top, foot); photo David Walker Micscape: p. 105; photos Jon Wilson p. 12; photos Kenn Wingle: pp. 32, 84; from George Wither, *A collection of Emblemes, Ancient and Moderne* . . . (London, 1635): p. 61; photos © Zoological Society of London: pp. 9 (from L. O. Howard, *The House-Fly, Disease-Carrier: An account of Its Dangerous Activities and of the Means of Destroying It* (New York, 1911), 49 (from Edward Donovan, *The Natural History of British Insects, Explaining Them in Their Several States . . .*, London: Rivington, 1803–13, vol. 14, 1810), 53 (from Donovan, vol. XI, 1810), 56 top (from James Samuelson and J. Braxton-Hicks, *Humble Creatures: The Earthworm and the Common Housefly . . .* (London, 1858), 63 (from Donovan, vol. 14, 1810), 70 (from August Johann Rösel von Rosenhof, *Der Monathlich-herausgebenen Insecten-Belustigung . . .*, 4 vols, Nuremberg, 1746–61), 87 (from John Curtis, *British Entomology; being illustrations and descriptions of the genera of insects found in Great Britain and Ireland: containing coloured figures from nature of the most rare and beautiful species, and in many instances of the plants upon which they are found*, London, 1823–40, vol 8, 1831), 88 (from Jacob Schaeffer, *Elementa Entomologica, cum appendice: Einleitung in die Insectenkenntnis . . .*, Regensberg, 1778), 92 (from Ulysse Aldrovandi, *De animalibus insectis libri septem cum Singulorum Iconibus ad Viuum Expressis*, Bologna, 1638), 94 (from Donovan, vol. 13, 1810), 135 (from John Swammerdam, *The Book of Nature, or The History of Insects*, London, 1758), 136 (from Francesco Redi, *Experimenta circa generationem insectorum ad nobilissimum virum carolum dati*, Amsterdam, 1671), 153 (from James R. Duncan, *Introduction to Entomology . . .*, Edinburgh, 1840), 155 (from Moses Harris, *An Exposition of English Insects, including the several classes of Neuroptera, Hymenoptera, & Diptera, or bees, flies, & Libellulae,*

London, 1702), 174 (James Samuelson and J. Braxton-Hicks, *Humble Creatures. The Earthworm and the Common Housefly . . .*, London, 1858).

Index